Christmas '89.

C000089146

A TASTE OF
SCOTCH

*An engraving of Sir Edwin Landseer's painting
"The Illicit Still in the Highlands" — 1829*

A TASTE OF
SCOTCH
DEREK COOPER

ANDRE DEUTSCH

First published in Great Britain 1989
by André Deutsch Limited
105−106 Great Russell Street London WC1

Copyright © 1989 Derek Cooper

British Library Cataloguing in Publication Data
Cooper, Derek, *1925−*
    A taste of scotch
    1. Scotch whiskies
    I. Title
    641.2'52

    ISBN 0-233-98460-7
Printed in Hong Kong

Contents

Acknowledgements — 6

Preface — 7

The Early Days — 9

Making It — 22

Distillers and Blenders — 31

Distilleries — 39

Paying For It — 57

The Tasting of It — 61

The Drinking of It — 72

Whisky and the Traveller — 86

Whisky and the Arts — 95

Whisky and Royalty — 100

Whisky and Religion — 104

Whisky as Medicine — 107

Toddies — 114

Deoch-an-Doruis — 117

WHITE HORSE INN.

Acknowledgements

The editor and publishers would like to thank the following for permitting the reproduction of copyright material in this book;

Barrie & Jenkins Ltd for the extract from *Four Absentees* by Rayner Heppenstall;

Mrs Valda Grieve and Martin Brian O'Keeffe Ltd for 'In Fancy I Drink Once Again' by Hugh MacDiarmid;

In Britain magazine for the extract from an article by William Foster;

Norman MacCaig and Chatto & Windus/The Hogarth Press for 'The Ballade of Good Whisky' from *Collected Poems*;

Macmillan Publishers Ltd for the extract from *Recollections of Three Reigns* by Sir Frederick Ponsonby;

New Scientist magazine for the extract from an article by Colin Tudge;

The Scotsman for the extract from articles by Anthony Troon;

The Society of Authors as literary representative of the Estate of Sir Compton Mackenzie for the extract from *My Life and Times*;

Souvenir Press Ltd for the extracts from *Whisky and Scotland* by Neil M. Gunn;

The *Sunday Telegraph Magazine* for the extract from an article by P. J. Kavanagh;

Times Newspapers Ltd for the article by Alan Hamilton from *The Times*, 17th September 1983, © Times Newspapers Ltd 1983.

We would also like to thank the many whisky enthusiasts who contributed to the success of this book and the Scotch whisky houses who laid open their libraries and files: United Distillers, Wm. Grant & Sons, Lang Brothers, Charles Mackinlay, Macdonald & Muir, Matthew Gloag, Seagram Distillers, White Horse Distillers, Macallan-Glenlivet, Arthur Bell and John Haig.

Preface

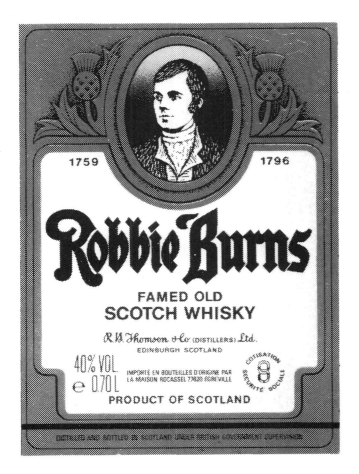

'You'll have a wee sensation,' says the Hebridean bank manager putting the cap on his pen and moving to a pine cupboard beside the hat stand in the corner.

'You'll take a small refreshment,' says the lady of the house bustling in with a tray.

They are both talking not of tea or sherry but of the strong water of life which has moved beyond its role as a mere beverage to become a ritual part of the Scottish way of life. Whisky.

It's not only freedom that whisky goes with, nor Burns' Night suppers, weddings and burials. It has suffused the ethos of Scotland to a degree unequalled by any liquor in any other culture.

The Scots have had not so much a love affair with uisge beatha as an infatuation on an epic scale. The English may sing about glorious beer but they have diluted their loyalties over the centuries with mead and cider, gin and port. The Scot has pursued his native drink with single-minded enthusiasm; he has pickled his wit and humour in it and elevated it into a national symbol with international appeal.

A few Hogmanays ago I saw the New Year in with a glass or two of The Glenlivet, high up in Darjeeling under the moon-drenched shadow of Kanchenjunga, and I thought at the time what a suitable and universal drink it was. Some weeks later coincidence directed me to some lines of David Daiches, recalling another Indian Hogmanay 'sitting on a bed in a hotel room in Agra with two friends and a bottle of Glenlivet after visiting the Taj Mahal by moonlight'.

He went on to suggest that the proper drinking of whisky is more than indulgence: 'It is a toast to civilization, a tribute to the continuity of culture, a manifesto of man's determination to use the resources of nature to refresh mind and body and enjoy to the full the sense with which he has been endowed.'

If this book celebrates anything it is the continuity of whisky in the cultural and social life of Scotland; in sickness and in health, in mirth and sorrow. Sir John Barleycorn has always been on hand.

The Scottish genius for converting barley into the world's pre-eminent spirit — an art not a science, they say — has inspired poets, novelists, songwriters, journalists and the journeymen of the advertising world. Whisky has in it an infinite capacity to speed the pen to florid heights of hyperbole, much of which is no doubt deeply regretted the morning after.

There's a little of that here; there's tartanry, prose as purple as late summer heather, and dreadful verse. But serious stuff too, for whisky is a serious thing. Not to be taken lightly and never with lemonade!

DEREK COOPER

Fall of the Clyde at Stonebyres

The Early Days

Nobody quite knows when or where the first cask of whisky was distilled in Scotland. They had been making aqua vitae *from barley since the fifteenth century, perhaps earlier. The churlish suggest that the inspiration came, along with Christianity, from Ireland, but, even if that is so, it was in the Highlands that the real spirit of Scotland was born. There the early days of illicit distillation were as swashbuckling and as romantic as anything from the pages of Robert Louis Stevenson.*

The copper worm concealed in the burn, the unlawful wisp of smoke rising from the whisky bothy, were signals both of rebellion and independence. As the smugglers passed on their ponies with a jingle of harness in the night there wasn't a soul that wished them harm. Old men in their dotage recalled the exhilaration of those wild days and the pitched battles between the smugglers and the revenue men.

The stills were often very primitive affairs, hidden in some quiet corner and artfully camouflaged from prying eyes. There was no stigma in pursuing this unlawful calling because the law itself was regarded as being unjust, if not iniquitous. John Stein, one of the early pioneers of the continuous still who was bankrupted by the industry of the smugglers, told a government enquiry in 1798 that illicit distillation 'spread itself over the whole face of the country and in every island from Orkney to Jura. There are many who practise this art who are ignorant of every other, and there are distillers who boast that they make the best possible Whiskey, who cannot read or write and who carry on this manufacture in parts of the country where the use of the plough is unknown and the face of the Exciseman is never seen.'

When whisky eventually came with some natural reluctance out of the heather it was like a laying down of

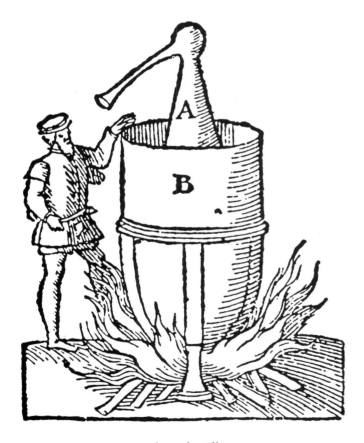

An early still

arms; indeed the Excise Act of 1823 had as numbing an affect on the native resistance movement as the Disarming Act of 1716. If Culloden finally buried the Jacobite dream, then the introduction of more liberal duties on malt were equally effective in unmanning the spirit of freebooting defiance.

So potent is the memory of those heroic days of whisky and freedom that there are many who regret their passing and not a few who believe, in the perverse way that some still hanker after a flat earth, that in remote parts of the Highlands and Islands old men are even now working clandestine stills. Stories are told about these freelancers of the glens and the superior taste and flavour of their moonlight mountain dew.

If you persevere you will actually meet people who claim to have tasted the stuff. It's marvellous, they will tell you, just like the good old whisky of the past. But what did that really taste like? By all accounts the stills the smugglers used were so primitive that they allowed all the undesirable oils and acids to pass over with the alcohol into the worm. Today whisky must by law be matured in oak for a minimum of three years, a period which allows any undesirable constituents of the raw spirit to be removed slowly by evaporation and oxidation. In the old days they often distilled one night and sold the next. Crudely made and full of congenerics, the illegal uisge must have had the kick of a Highland stallion. But it was cheap and duty free. Everyone with a free elbow was joyfully knocking back this fiery stuff that went like a torchlight procession down the throat and had never paid a pennyworth of tax. Each dram taken was a liquid protest against the English and the 'outlandish race that filled the Stuart's throne'. It was not only a pleasure to drink the stuff . . . it was a patriotic duty!

A distillery in 1729

*Early 18th-century woodcut of John Barleycorn,
the personification of malt liquor*

The witness deponed unanimously that they saw the caldron on the fyre, and a stand reiking and that they heard the goodwife say 'the lasse has put on the caldron and played some afterwort' and she knew not whether her caldron was before on the fyre on a Sabbath day and had she been at home it should not have been done (for she was byt presentlie cam'd from Alloway Church). So it being only some pynts of small drink played by a servant lass naither maister nor mistresse accessarie to it upon engadgment of Christian carriage for the future, rebuked before the Session.

ROBERT HAIG, SUMMONED TO APPEAR BEFORE THE KIRK SESSION OF ST NINIAN'S PARISH CHURCH, JANUARY 1655 FOR WORKING HIS STILL ON THE SABBATH

The following story, told me by the late Rev. John Fraser, Kiltarlity, shows the persistence which characterized the smugglers and the leniency with which illicit distillation was regarded by the better classes. While the Rev. Mr Fraser was stationed at Erchless, shortly before the Disruption, a London artist, named McIan*. *The Highland Whisky Still* was exhibited in the Scottish Royal Academy in 1843 came north to take sketches for illustrating a history of the Highlands, then in preparation. He was very anxious to see a smuggling bothy at work, and applied to Mr Robertson, factor for The Chisholm. 'If Sandy MacGruar is out of jail,' said the factor, 'we shall have no difficulty in seeing a bothy.' Enquiries were made, Sandy was at large, and, as usual, busy smuggling. A day was fixed for visiting the bothy, and MacIan, accompanied by Mr Robertson, the factor, and Dr Fraser of Kerrow, both Justices of the Peace, and by the Rev. John Fraser, was admitted into Sandy's sanctuary. The sketch having been finished, the factor said, '*Nach eil dad agad Alasdair?*' (Haven't you got something, Sandy?) Sandy having removed some heather, produced a small keg. As the four worthies were quaffing the real mountain dew, the Rev. Mr Fraser remarked, 'This would be a fine haul for the gaugers—the sooner we go the better.' It was the same Sandy who, on seeing a body of Excise officers defile round the shoulder of a hill, began counting them *aon, dha, tri*, but on counting seven, his patience became exhausted and he exclaimed, '*A Tighearna, cuir sgrios orra!*' — Lord destroy them!

IAN MACDONALD

* Robert Ronald McIan (1803–56).

At our request, Mr McGregor, Jun., took us to see the various haunts of the smugglers, who in days gone by were pretty numerous in the district. He first directed us to the double-arched cavern, dug deep into the hill, fifty yards from the distillery, in which at one time a noted band of smugglers carried on their operations, but it has since been demolished. It possessed an underground spring, wherein the little coil of worm, which condensed the precious spirit, was laid, and at a lower level it dripped into a receiver, made out of an earthen jar some two feet high, with a wooden lid thereon. The little copper still stood on a furnace made with the loose stones that had fallen from the rock behind, and the mashtun had originally been a wash-tub. The place was totally dark, and no light was ever permitted except that which came from the furnace fire. One night the revenue officers made a raid on the place, and knowing the desperate men they had to deal with, were all well armed. On their arrival they crept stealthily through the narrow entrance to the cave, following the informer, who knew the place well. Meanwhile the smugglers, unconscious of the close proximity of their enemies, were scattered about the cavern, some sleeping, others smoking, and one or two looking after the distilling operations. One of their number opened the furnace door to replenish the fire, and the momentary flash of light revealed to his comrades the figures of the officers stealing upon them. With great presence of mind he instantly unhooked the pipe which connected the furnace with a concealed chimney in the roof, and then fired off his pistol at the nearest enemy. The noise alarmed the gang who escaped from the cave under the cover of the dense smoke

emitted from the open furnace. The officers were dumbfounded, and almost choked, but the informer quickly replaced the chimney-pipe, and as soon as the smoke had dispersed, the officers lighted their lamps from the furnace fire, and proceeded to demolish the place. They broke up the still, worm and vessels, kicked the debris and loose stone into the well, annexed a few kegs of whisky, and departed with one of their comrades slightly wounded. This scare broke up and scattered the notorious gang and since that time there has been very little smuggling in this district.

ALFRED BARNARD AT BALMENACH DISTILLERY

Smuggling in the Highlands—the capture of an illicit whisky still, from an engraving of 1833

We frequently quitted the coast in order to go through the villages, built on tops of hills which bound it; the inhabitants, little accustomed to see strangers, took us for custom–house officers; thus we saw them flying before us, and shutting up, at our approach, all their huts in which they had established private distilleries of whisky, which are prohibited by law.

Arriving at the foot of the rocks, at a distance from all habitation, we stumbled by accident on the depot of all the contraband. In a small cavern, the entrance into which was covered with briars, were ranged thirty or forty casks of whisky, destined to be transported during the night on board a vessel anchored at a little distance. Some very ancient iron lances were lying at the mouth of the grotto; they were the arms used by the smugglers in case of attack. Raising our eyes, we perceived, on the top of the rocks a troop of men who, with eager looks, were attentively watching all our movements. These were the proprietors of the whisky. We hastened to calm their uneasiness, by retiring without touching the depot; but no doubt these unfortunate people, seeing their enterprise discovered, expected their casks to be seized before the close of the day.

L. A. NECKER DE SAUSSURE, A VOYAGE TO THE HEBRIDES, 1822

There was a romance about it. The still was generally placed in some secluded spot, in the ravine of a Highland burn, or screened by waving birch and natural wood, so that the smoke of the fire could scarcely be observed. There were scouts placed around, often three or four savage-looking men, sometimes women and boys.

JOSEPH MITCHELL

The Smugglers' Cave

Just over a hundred years ago [circa 1820] there lived on the Heights of Strathpeffer one John Macdonald. He was then about forty years of age. For many years John had kept two smuggling bothies going alternately. One was in *Coire Bhothain* and the other at the *Leth-allt* near *Cnoc na Bainnse*. He always played a lone hand, thus avoiding the usual pitfall of the smuggler – a babbling confederate. So that not a breath of suspicion blew his way, and all might have continued well had not a gamekeeper by an unlucky chance one day actually walked through the roof of the *Coire Bhothain* bothy and discovered John redhanded at his hobby. He was an unfriendly gamekeeper that; he lodged information with the authorities at Dingwall.

After trial John was duly sentenced to be detained for a period of six weeks as an unwilling guest of His Majesty King William IV. John's wife walked to Dingwall every other day bringing food for the prisoner. A fortnight went by without incident. Then John had a brain-wave. The old jailer was well known to favour the cup that cheers; in fact he was possessed of a chronic and insatiable thirst – and on that John gambled – and won.

During the remaining four weeks of the sentence there was observed a gentleman's agreement whereby every evening after dark John's cell door was unlocked. John then proceeded by a quiet route to the *Cnoc na Bainnse* bothy and there worked strenuously and in complete safety until returning dawn warned him it was time to make for his prison again; which he did – bringing with him in liquid form the price of the old jailer's complicity.

As John's son put it to me, 'The safest smuggling my father ever did was that time he was in Dingwall Jile.'

COLIN MACDONALD

During his 28 years of harassing those who felt that whisky and freedom were synonymous Malcolm Gillespie (1779—1827) the most persistent Exciseman in the history of Scotland, sustained 42 wounds. He impounded 6,535 gallons of whisky; 407 stills; 165 horses; 85 carts and 62,400 gallons of the barley wash from which uisge *beatha* was distilled. He was hanged for uttering forged bills on 16 November 1827.

Gillespie, who was for some time located in the Skene district to intercept the hill smugglers on their way to Aberdeen. He had the assistance of a trained dog, who seized the horses by the nose and made them tumble the whisky kegs off their backs. Gillespie and his men also used bludgeons, pistols and swords, and there were many serious cuts, bruises and broken limbs. Gillespie himself was nearly mauled to death more than once by these men from the hills.

DR ALEXANDER, *NORTHERN RURAL SKETCHES*

On a day in the early part of the nineteenth century a band of smugglers from nearby Braemar set out for Aberdeen with the view of selling their whisky. As they had no less than ten cart-loads they were accompanied by a number of friends to assist them in dealing with the exciseman. There was no opposition till Culter was reached. By that time thick darkness had settled down, and heavy thunder showers fell. It was a fearful night and the smugglers thought the excisemen would not be out. The advanced scouts had reached Stonegavel Inn where a bright light in a window arrested attention. Approaching cautiously, they peered into the room, and beheld their relentless foe, Malcolm Gillespie, seated at a table on which lay two pistols. They retraced their steps, but found that Gillespie's men — who were concealed near by — were already attacking the smuggling party. For some time there was a terrific battle. The smugglers were more numerous than the gaugers, but not so well armed, their cudgels being less effective than their opponents' sabres. The battle was long and determined, the men on both sides fighting like demons. In the end the smugglers were vanquished and their whisky fell into the hands of the excisemen. Many on both sides were very seriously wounded and one smuggler was killed outright.

JOHN A. HENDERSON

When a boy in Brechin, I was quite familiar with the appearance and on-goings of the Highland smugglers. They rode on Highland ponies, carrying on each side of their small, shaggy but brave and hardy steeds, a small cask or 'keg' as it was called, of illicit whisky, manufactured amid the wilds of Aberdeenshire or the glens of the Grampians. They took up a position on some commanding eminence during the day, where they could, as from a watch-tower, descry the distant approach of the enemy, the exciseman or gauger: then, when night fell, every man to horse, descending the mountains only six miles from Brechin, they scoured the plains, rattled into the villages and towns, disposing of their whisky to agents they had everywhere . . .

I have seen a troop of thirty of them riding in Indian file, and in broad day, through the streets of Brechin, after they had succeeded in disposing of their whisky, and as they rode leisurely along, beating time with their formidable cudgels on the empty barrels to the great amusement of the public and the mortification of the excisemen, who had nothing for it but to bite their nails and stand, as best they could, the raillery of the smugglers and the laughter of the people.

REV. THOMAS GUTHRIE

When the smugglers have a large smuggling adventure ready, about Callander, Crieff, or any-where on the borders of the line, having established a telegraphic communication betwixt Stirling and these places, a person is stationed at Ballangich, the hill at the west end of Stirling Castle, who, having watched the motions of the Excise Officers, and seen and found out what road they take, he gives a certain whistle, a sign, which is heard and transmitted by other persons stationed at proper distances all the way, and by these means they communicate the information in a very few minutes from Stirling to Callander, or any like distance. Having obtained this notice, they immediately dispatch one or two of their worst horses, with two anchors [small casks of ten gallons capacity] upon each; these go directly in the way of the Officers and when they fall in with them, make a great feigned resistance, but at last after a great deal ado, they are taken and carried off by the Officers in triumph, who congratulate themselves on being very successful, and return home well pleased with their night's excursion, but while they are so occupied and amused, the smugglers run down twenty, thirty, or forty times this quantity with perfect safety by other roads.

THE COURIER, LONDON, 14 JULY 1804

When the Glenlivet company celebrated its 150th anniversary in August 1974 at Minmore the Chairman of George & J. G. Smith was Captain 'Bill' Smith Grant who was able to trace his distilling and family background back through six generations to around 1747 and the John Gow who had been 'out' with the Prince in the '45. To escape retribution Gow anglicized his name to Smith, moved from his native Braes of Mar, and settled down to farm near Tomintoul where he began illicitly distilling.

Captain Bill Smith Grant MC DL

In smuggling as in poaching, there is a spirit of adventure and hazard, which has a charm for the minds of the peasantry. An escape or a successful resistance is remembered, and related as an heroic achievement; men encourage each other and a fraternity of feeling is produced among them by a sense of common danger.

EIGHTEENTH CENTURY TRAVELLER

OLD SCOTCH NECTAR
A & R. Vannan, GLASGOW.

Even so late as then, say 1820, one would go a long way before one met a person who shrank from smuggling. My father never tasted any but smuggled whisky, and when every mortal that called for him — they were legion daily — had a dram instantly poured into him, the ankers of whisky emptied yearly must have been numerous indeed.

When I was young everyone I met from my father downwards, even our clergy, either made, bought, sold or drank cheerfully, smuggled liquor.

On the watershed between Strath Bran and Fannich, I have been in a bothy with regularly built, low stone walls, watertight heather thatch, iron pipes leading cold spring water to the still-rooms and such an array of casks, tubs, etc., as told that gaugers never troubled their owners.

DR JOHN MACKENZIE, UNCLE OF OSGOOD HANBURY MACKENZIE OF INVEREWE

The Excise Men

This lovely wooded glen is a favourite resort of tourists and artists, but in olden days smugglers located themselves here, where, defying the law, they made a celebrated Whisky which was in great demand. Tradition says that there is a smuggler imprisoned in the heart of the hill, who is kept in durance vile by the avenging spirit of a revenue officer whose life he took. He is allowed to come forth once a year at midnight, on the anniversary of the day upon which the crime was committed, and should he then happen to meet the spirit of the comrade who betrayed him to the officers of the law, the spell would be broken and he released.

ALFRED BARNARD AT GLENDARROCH

Many smugglers constituted a sort of recognized corporation, claiming a rank second to that of the landowners, and bearing themselves as the *petite noblesse* of the community. In church they occupied as a body the front pew of the gallery which was spoken of as the 'smugglers loft' and this not sneeringly but with a feeling of respect. The illegality of their employment was forgotten or disregarded in a neighbourhood where persons of all ranks were openly and unscrupulously their customers . . . The smugglers dwelt in excellent houses, wore fine clothes, rode showy horses and exercised a cordial hospitality.

PROFESSOR WALKER

James Macgregor combined the arduous task of hacking farms out of peat, bog and heather with the more lucrative sideline of illicit distilling.

Soon after the passing of the Act of 1823 he received a visit from the nearest excise officer. Their talk was friendly and began with a generous dram of pure malt whisky. When these preliminaries were finished to the satisfaction of both men, the excise officer mentioned shyly that he had his duty to perform and had better have a look round. Out went the two men to inspect the farm. All went well until they came to a rough stone building with a mill-wheel and a mill-lade by its side.

'What will that be?' asks the excise officer.

'Oh,' says my great-grandfather, 'that'll just be the peat-shed.'

Nothing more was said, and the two men went back to the house for another dram and a talk about the crops and the prospects of the harvest. Then as the gauger took his leave, he said quietly:

Cutting the peats

'If I were you, Mr Macgregor, I'd just take out a licence for yon peat-shed.'

SIR ROBERT BRUCE LOCKHART

Somewhere on the Braes of Angus at the head of Glenquiech is buried a whisky still. It was bequeathed to my father by 'Rashiebog' when I was an infant. He had a map of the location. When, full of years and very tired, the Minister of Memus passed on, I found no trace of this heritage. It is possible that my father washed his hands of it. A strict teetotaller, though he enjoyed making wines and liqueurs, he may have resented the suggestion that he might take to making Mountain Dew. I wish he had treasured this inheritance. I would have liked to have had it as an heirloom of the days when, when Scotland willed she found a way.

ELIZABETH CRAIG

About 18 months ago I was in a pub near here and this guy was very drunk and he was making rude remarks about modern whisky distillers — the stuff wasn't nearly as good as the stuff he used to make in his way. It turned out that this character had been making illicit whisky in years gone by and he had two accomplices. The first guy did the malting — he procured the barley, possibly from his own croft, and he malted it. Then he ground it and transferred his grist to partner number two who mashed and fermented it. When the fermentation was finished he put the wash into some old-fashioned milk churns and took it to number three, who was the chap telling the story. He did the distilling and his bothy was somewhere on Ben Rinnes. They were never caught and they reckon the reason was the three different departments were miles apart.

SPEYSIDE DISTILLERY MANAGER 1980

Making It

It is an old wife's tale that you never get a decent cup of tea from a new pot. It is an old distillers' belief that you never get good whisky from a new still—it takes time for the copper to acquire the patina of perfection.

'Nonsense,' said a brewer of one of the finest malts in the islands, 'they all say these things. There are men who make good whisky and men who can't make good whisky. Give me any still and I'll make it work!'

For thirty years now I have been wandering round distilleries and listening to the men who make malt whisky. And I always come away none the wiser. What makes Glenfiddich so different from its neighbour, Balvenie? Why is there so much variation between one Islay whisky and another? Some swear by tall stills, some by short; others like their water to be peat-soft or calcium-hard. There are those who swear by coal-fired stills and others who believe that steam coils are best. Lightly peated malt, heavily peated malt; short maturation, long maturation.

From my notebooks let me extract five quotations from five men who are responsible for producing five very distinctive malts:

It is neither an art nor is it a science. It is knowing when to cut; knowing when to do all sorts of things.

At the end of the day it's all to do with humidity; you can't make good whisky in a dry climate. You need moisture and the right temperatures.

The Glenlivet/Seagrams

The barley is all important. Good grain makes good whisky. It's nothing do with anything else — except maybe the yeast and the way you age your spirit, of course, and look after it and things like that.

I would put it down to the water first and foremost; then the shape of the still, the angle of the lyne arm and the skill of the man in the stillhouse. And then the oak — the cask, that makes all the difference.

I'll tell you. A good mash, a long slow distillation, a long ageing and then a good nose and palate to make sure it's all come together.

So it's just a few things — and it's all things. Standing on the edge of the sea in Islay there are those who detect the hint of marine iodine in Laphroaig. In Skye they say it's the peat that makes Talisker. The way the wind blows is important too . . . or so those with a sense of humour will tell you. A lot of this is nonsense; an irrational respect for ritual, custom and the wisdom of the past. Or is it?

Roderick Mackenzie of Wester Ross who used to make whisky at Linkwood distillery near Elgin is said to have been so concerned about the continuity of his whisky production that he frowned when even a spider's web was brushed away in the tun room. Everything played its part in the alchemy.

At each place where he halted on his monumental pilgrimage to every distillery in the British Isles in 1887 Alfred Barnard enquired of the owner what it was that made each malt so unique. He noted that the very finest malts were produced either on the seashore or on the side of the mountains.

'We must', he was told by the distillers, 'have plenty of water power and good water, so we select the banks of a quickly-flowing stream. Then again we use home-grown barley and only peat of the finest quality for drying the malt; also we believe that a good climate and pure air are indispensable in the production of a delicate spirit like whisky.'

A hundred years later waterpower is unimportant — the National Grid runs through every glen. Barley comes from Australia or East Anglia; it is processed mechanically in central maltings. The distiller himself may well be a townsman with a BSc and a

The Glenlivet / Seagrams

calculator in his pocket. The process of converting the imported malt into uisge *is likely to be controlled from an electronic console.*

But some magic remains. They cannot duplicate whisky anywhere else in the world. Nobody makes whisky like the Scots.

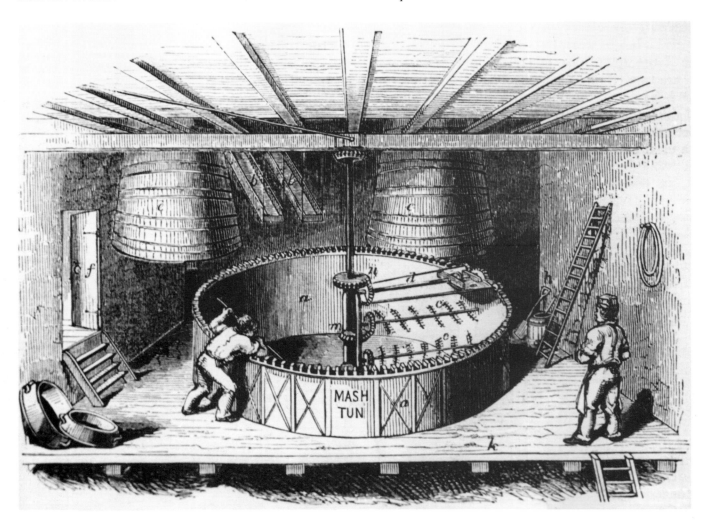

Down round the southern corner of the dun there was a field of barley all ripened by the sun. In a small wind it echoed faintly the sound of the ocean; at night it sighed and rustled as the earth mother thought over things, not without a little anxiety. It was cut and harvested and a sheaf offered in thanksgiving; flailed and winnowed; until the ears of grain remained in a heap of pale gold: The bread of life.

In simple ways the grain was prepared and set to ferment: the fermented liquor was then boiled, and as the stream came off it was by happy chance condensed against some cold surface.

And lo! This condensation of the stream from the greenish-yellow fermented gruel is clear as crystal. It is purer than any water from any well. When cold, it is colder to the fingers than ice.

A marvellous transformation. A perfect water — but in the mouth — what is this? The gums tingle, the throat burns, down into the belly fire passes, and thence outward to the fingertips, to the feet, and finally to the head.

And then — and then — the head goes up. The film dissolves from the eyes; they glisten. He abruptly laughs and jumps to his feet; as abruptly pauses to look over himself with a marvellous scrutiny. He tries the muscles of his arms. They are full of such energy that one fist shoots out; then the other. A right and left. His legs have the same energy. He begins to dance with what is called primitive abandon. Clearly it was not water he had drunk; it was life, *it was life*.

One night in the tun-room a large back was having a fearsome battle with the switchers. The old brewer, a close friend of mine, was growing anxious, for the vessel was swaying on her bottom, with sides heaving.

Is she at her worst?' I cried.

'Not yet.'

'At what degree will she be at her worst?'

'At twenty-one, like a woman,' he answered.

NEIL GUNN

At Aberfeldy distillery, Perthshire one of 40 malt whisky distilleries within the Distillers Company, a mixture of malf grist and hot water enters the mash-tun. The mixture 'wort' is then fermented by the addition of yeast.

To appreciate the difficulties of blending, the layman should experiment on his own account. He may take half a dozen of the finest highland malts, those from the classic distilleries, mix them together and add any proportion he chooses of grain whisky. The result will almost certainly be a blend that is totally unacceptable, one in which all the subtle distinctive qualities of the different malts have been entirely lost. The truth is that a good blend requires whiskies of less pronounced character just as much as it needs the classic malts.

DONALD MACKINLAY

Scotch Whisky is a mystery, a magic of locality. The foreigner may import not only Scottish barley, but Scottish water, Scottish distilling apparatus, and set a Scot to work on them, but the glory evaporates: it will not travel.

IVOR BROWN

It is a widely held belief in the Highlands that the best whisky is made from water which comes off granite through peat.

The making of Scotch whisky is cookery, but cookery on a grand scale and with an entire economy at stake. It is precise and understood in the sense that men in white coats describe in polysyllables everything that's going on. But the job of the men in white coats is not to take the process apart and reassemble it, in pastiche form, as the brewers did with beer, but simply to see that the traditional, empirical process goes smoothly on its way. Cookery, precisely monitored, is the modern art of whisky making.

Whisky is more than half pure water. Forty per cent, by volume, is ethanol. If the aim of the whisky maker were to produce alcohol in aqueous solution then all the rest, the hundreds of higher alcohols, esters and phenols would be seen as impurities. As it is, the whole exercise, from the growing of the barley to the search for sherry barrels in darkest Spain, is designed specifically to produce those 'impurities': huge areas of land, a marvellous variety of buildings and machines; thousands of people and vast sums of money, designed to ensure that just a few parts per million of some recondite ester find their way into suitable company in a nice clean bottle, with ethanol and water.

COLIN TUDGE, *NEW SCIENTIST* 1981

WP Lowrie bottle washing department, 1909

The grain consumed in distillation is not wholly lost in human food. It has been ascertained that as much milk, beef, pork, or other animal food can be raised from the draff and dreg, after the spirit is extracted, as could have been produced upon the land on which the barley grew, had it been sown with grass and thrown into pasture.

1813 **REPORT**

Highland Park
The most northern Scotch whisky distillery in the world.

Having done justice to the Still House . . . we noticed a peculiarly shaped timber building, which our guide informed us is called the 'Heather House'. Here heather is stored, which has been gathered in the month of July, when the blossom is fully set. It is carefully cut off near the root, and tied into small faggots of about a dozen branches. One or two of these faggots are used with the peat in drying the malt every time the fire is made up, and imparts a delicate flavour of its own to the malt, rendering

Highland Park Whisky unlike any other made in the kingdom. To convince us of this, a few sprigs, well covered with dried blossoms, were thrown into an open *chauffeur* with a small quantity of peat, and we must confess that we detected a most pronounced odour, and quite different from the peat when used alone. We have only seen the heather used in three other distilleries in the whole kingdom.

ALFRED BARNARD

The smaller the still the finer the product.

OLD SMUGGLER'S BELIEF

Newly distilled whisky possesses a harsh flavour. Before it can be drunk it must, therefore, undergo a further process, called 'maturation'. It is put into oak casks which are placed in cool warehouses, where they remain for three to ten years or more.

Three main groups of reactions take place. The first is a not fully understood intra-molecular rearrangement of the various components of the whisky itself—it is known, for example, that a proportion of some of the alcohols become converted into esters; the second is the slow extraction from the oak wood itself of certain of the complex molecules of which it is composed; and the third group of changes is the interaction of these compounds extracted from the cask with certain components of the whisky.

DR MAGNUS PYKE

We were aye discussing what gave whisky its character . . . We never agreed; I do not think that anyone has ever agreed. One distiller . . . held that the excellent quality of his spirit was due to the shape of the head of the low-wine still, that retained or sent over certain of the furfurals and essential oils. It could be. Anyway his still was always breaking down to the danger of our immortal souls, but he steadfastly refused to install a new plant lest he spoil his whisky; and when he was finally forced to build a new still he called in expert coppersmiths from Alloa to copy exactly the old still, in every bolt, in every joint, in every curve, and, what is more, in every patch. And he held that he proved his theory, for his whisky did retain its character—a rather negative proof we thought.

MAURICE WALSH

Their plenty of corn was such, as disposed the natives to brew several sorts of liquor as common usquebaugh, another called trestarig, *id est,* aquavitae, three times distilled, which is strong and hot; and this by the natives is called usquebaugh-baul, *id est* usquebaugh, which at first taste affects all the members of the body; two spoonfuls of this last liquor is a sufficient dose; and if any man exceed this, it would presently stop his breath, and endanger his life.

MARTIN MARTIN

Set half a dozen samples of Scotch whisky in front of a group of distillers and they will argue long into the night, not so much about the merits of the whisky but about whether by some change in the choice of grain, the timing of the process or the length or method of maturation, a different result might have been achieved.

S. RUSSELL GRANT, GLENLIVET DISTILLERIES

Very many persons think they can blend whisky, and that it is just a matter of throwing a few brands together. The manipulation of whiskies requires as much care as the most delicate wines. Mountain air, peat moss of the richest quality, pure water from the hills and the best Scotch malt are absolute requirements for the manufacture of Highland whisky, in order to ensure the pronounced characteristics so highly valued by the experienced blender; and it is the development of these by age which gives bouquet and relish to a fine blend.

ALFRED BARNARD

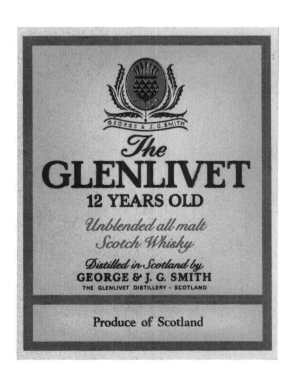

The
GLENLIVET
12 YEARS OLD
Unblended all malt
Scotch Whisky
Distilled in Scotland by
GEORGE & J. G. SMITH
THE GLENLIVET DISTILLERY · SCOTLAND

Produce of Scotland

In 1785 a proposal was made to collect the duty on the manufacture of spirits in Scotland by way of licence, to be paid annually, for every still according to its size, at a fixed rate, per gallon, in lieu of all other duties.

The London Distillers, men the most experienced in their profession, who agreed to the rate of the licence on the gallon, supposed to be equivalent to the former duties, declared themselves, from experience satisfied that the time for working stills to an advantage was limited to an extent perfectly well known and that whoever exceeded those limits would infallibly lose upon his materials and the quality of the goods, what he gained in point of time: and, in conformity to their opinion, the duty was in 1786, settled upon the supposition that stills could be discharged about *seven times a week*.

Two years after this, in a memorial presented to the Lords Commissioners of the Treasury, the same men alleged that the Scotch distillers had, by the ingenuity of their contrivances, found means to discharge their still *forty times a week*, and from a report of the Lords Commissioners of the Treasury, in 1789, it appears that a forty-three gallon still was brought to such a degree of perfection, as to be discharged in two minutes and three quarters; almost *twenty-two times an hour*.

This mode of levying duty on the bulk of the still is discontinued and the duty is charged on the quantity of spirit produced.

JAMES MITCHELL

Notwithstanding the quantity of bear* raised, there is often a sort of dearth; the inhabitants being mad enough to convert their bread into poison, distilling annually six thousand bolls of grain into whisky. The Duke of Argyle, the principal proprietor of this country takes great pains in discouraging the pernicious practice; and obliges all his tenants to enter into articles, to forfeit five pounds and the still in case they are detected in making this *liqueur d'enfer*; but the trade is so profitable that many persist in it to the great neglect of manufactures. Before this business got ground the women were accustomed to spin a great deal of yarn (for much flax is raised in these parts) but at present they employ themselves in distilling while their husbands are in the field.

THOMAS PENNANT IN THE MULL OF KINTYRE IN THE SUMMER OF 1772

* bere, a form of barley

I have seen a skilled tintometer operator carefully working out the amount of caramel colouring that goes into an eight-year-old (a very light colour this), a twelve-year-old (somewhat darker) and a twenty-year-old (darker still) blend, colouring the whisky according to its age to fool the consumer into believing that the darker it is the older. They say that the sweet, gooey caramel stuff that goes into the whisky is in too insignificant proportions to affect the taste, but in the case of the darker coloured whiskies I am not so sure.

DAVID DAICHES

I knew one small town with seven distilleries and I knew an expert who could distinguish the seven by bouquet alone. The seven distilleries were in one mile of Highland river; they used the same water, peat and malt, and the methods of brewing and distillation were identical, yet each spirit had its own individual bouquet. One, the best, mellowed perfectly in seven years; another, the least good, not a hundred yards away, was still liquid fire at the end of ten years.

MAURICE WALSH

One evening, before the last war, as the Managing Director of Macallan left the distillery he espied an employee draped over his bicycle in a ditch by the side of the road. He stopped and asked if he could be of assistance. To his surprise the body spoke: 'Aye, it's a funny thing the whisky sir — it pits you oan the road in a Humber Snipe, an' me aff it oan ma bike!'

WILLIE PHILLIPS, CHAIRMAN OF MACALLAN

Distillers and Blenders

DCL MALT EXTRACT

THE DISTILLERS COMPANY LTD

The Distillers Coy. Ltd
EDINBURGH.

It is in the interests of the working man, many of whom are not judges of whisky, that they should be protected from the young, cheap, fiery whisky which is offered. Experience teaches that most of the riotous and obstreperous conduct of drunks comes from the young and fiery spirit which is sold, while men who may over-indulge in old matured whisky become sleepy and stupid, but not in a fighting mood.

THE WORDS WERE ADDRESSED TO THE CHANCELLOR OF THE EXCHEQUER BY PETER 'WHITE HORSE' MACKIE, OPPOSING THE LLOYD GEORGE BUDGET

The finest plea ever made by a whisky distiller for compulsory temperance.

Sir Peter took over Lagavulin distillery on Islay in 1888 and with it the agency for nearby Laphroaig. Some time afterwards the owner of Laphroaig, Alexander Johnston, fell out with Mackie and Mackie cut off his water supply. Johnston sued White Horse for the restoration of his rights, won the case and refused to sell Mackie any more Laphroaig. Sir Peter — 'Restless Peter' as he was nicknamed — decided that he would make his own Laphroaig. He built two stills which were exact replicas of the ones in Laphroaig. He even went to the lengths of poaching the brewer from Laphroaig, but when the spirit came off the stills it was not Laphroaig. The water was the same, the barley the same, the peat the same but somehow Laphroaig refused to be duplicated.

I had tried repeatedly to open an account with the Associated Music Halls Companies in London, which were then controlled by a well-known figure — Mr Newsom Smith, the head of a large accountancy house and Chairman of the United Music Halls Company. This company comprised practically all the leading music halls of the time — the Pavilion, Metropolitan, Oxford, Canterbury and several others. I could see that it was a very fine opportunity to get a good advertisement for my whisky if I could get the account. It occurred to me one day that if I could manage to get Mr Newsom Smith to audit my accounts and prepare my yearly balance that I would in this way get in touch with the music halls . . . I need hardly say that I brought off the business that I desired and very soon my whisky was the dominant blend in all those London music halls.

JAMES BUCHANAN, FOUNDER OF JAMES BUCHANAN & CO., THE FIRST MAN TO PUT A WHITE LABEL ON A BLACK BOTTLE. IN TOP HAT AND WITH AN ORCHID IN HIS BUTTONHOLE, HE CUT A DASHING FIGURE IN VICTORIAN LONDON. 'THERE ARE FEW MORE IMPRESSIVE SIGHTS IN THE WORLD,' SAID SIR JAMES BARRIE, 'THAN A SCOTSMAN ON THE MAKE', AND HIS REMARK MIGHT HAVE BEEN TAILOR-MADE FOR THE SPLENDIDLY TAILORED BUCHANAN

Over the last half-century, the movement of Scotch away from the Scots has been unstoppable, and fewer than one-sixth of the distilleries remain in Scottish hands. Here is a roll-call of the movement since 1970:

Lochside Grain Distillery, Montrose, bought by Destilerias y Crianza de Whisky, of Spain; Aberlour Glenlivet and White Heather Distillers taken over by Pernod; Long John International sold by Schenley Industries Inc. of New York to Whitbreads, the English brewing combine; William Teachers and Sons taken over by Allied Brewers; Glenlivet Distillers taken over by Seagrams of Canada.

It is ironic that the companies who acquire Scotch distilleries continue to talk through their advertising of the drink and its place in Scotland's social tradition. They have bought the right to do this; but while the craft of distilling Scotch whisky will always belong to Scotland, the whisky increasingly belongs to someone else.

ANTHONY TROON, *THE SCOTSMAN*, DECEMBER 1978

A friend of mine was chairman of a little company producing Antiquary, a grand liqueur whisky. One of the founders, a Mr Hardie, had a very Victorian wife, who decided he was drinking too much whisky. Being canny, he said not a word, but arranged that Antiquary, which was then a typically dark whisky, would in future become very light. He drank as much as he had done heretofore, maybe a little more; she thought he was qualifying it well, and they lived happily together for many more years.

CEDRIC DICKENS

The "Johnnie Walker" cask expert testing the soundness of a cask

Madam, on 14th February last you called at my office and got one bottle whisky and two bottles brandy value 8/3 promising to call and pay it on a fortnight after. I was under the presumption that you were a lady and would keep your promise, although a stranger to me. If I do not hear from you before Friday first I will have a different opinion of your character and will take steps accordingly.

ARTHUR BELL WRITING TO MRS RODGER OF AUCHTERMUCHTY IN THE 1850s FROM HIS SHOP IN PERTH

There is little doubt that dilettantism is still widespread in the industry. The preponderance of traditional aristocratic owners may not cause much surprise. One of the principal achievements of the founder in this century of one of the largest and most successful of all the brand name whiskies, was the writing of a huge and definitive tome on gamekeeping, and a photograph of the modern head of a whisky house is still more likely to depict him fishing, shooting, or surrounded by dogs or horses, than in his distillery.

Such owners have always been, and are still, trained from birth to value tradition, continuity, and stability and to encourage others to the same values, partly, of course since it is upon these very features of life that their own continuing authority depends.

ROBERT HUMPHRIES, SENIOR DISTRICT MANAGER, CHARRINGTON, *HOSPITALITY*, MARCH 1980

During the Prohibition era, Francis Berry of Berry Bros was looking for a blend that he could sell in the legitimate Bahamas market. In the early 1920s he commissioned the Scottish artist James McBey to design a label. It was McBey who came up with the idea of using the name of the famous China tea clipper which had just been bought and restored to public view. Thus was Cutty Sark born in 1923. The fact that the ship, under full sail, bore a romantic resemblance to the Atlantic schooners engaged in rum-running from the West Indies to the USA did not detract from its success.

The tea clipper itself took its name from the witch in Burns' *Tam O'Shanter*, who wore a cutty sark — a short skirt.

Should Auld Acquaintance Be Forgot.

The founders of (Ardbeg) were the McDougalls, the last survivor of whom was Alexander McDougall who died in 1853. He was well known among the members of the spirit trade in Glasgow about fifty years ago, and his integrity and straightforwardness of character gained him the entire confidence of his friends and customers. He was liberal and benevolent, while his clannishness was intense. This Highland virtue he prominently exhibited on a certain occasion when he discovered in court that some unknown namesake was pronounced by the judge 'Guilty' and sentence of a fine or imprisonment was imposed. Mr McDougall interposed the statement 'that it was impossible that a McDougall could do anything wrong' and therefore he would pay the fine!

ALFRED BARNARD

"Why do you always insist on that particular brand of Whisky?"
"Because I believe in getting the best, and the best is

DEWAR'S "

THE FAMOUS "White Label" IS A MOST ZEST-GIVING BEVERAGE AT MEALS

Britannia & Eve for January, 1934

Dewar used to present the importunate with a card which read 'I have given up lending money for some time. But I don't mind having a drink. Make it Dewar's.'

DEWAR'S
THE SPIRIT OF THE SEAS
From the great blue deep came forth the Empire, boundless and free. Across the wide waters of all the Seas unceasingly pass men and ships binding more tightly the common bonds of a noble heritage. Not least amongst these ties is . . .
DEWAR'S

On meeting a woman at a dinner party who told him that her name was 'Porter-Porter with a hyphen' Tom Dewar replied, 'and mine is Dewar-Dewar with a syphon.'

Our new Moses to take us out of the wilderness of strenuous competition and lead us into the land flowing with respectable dividends.

THOMAS DEWAR APOSTROPHIZING WILLIAM ROSS, WHO IN 1925, AFTER 28 YEARS AS GENERAL MANAGER OF THE DISTILLERS COMPANY, BECAME ITS CHAIRMAN. IT WAS ROSS, KNOWN AS THE ABRAHAM LINCOLN OF THE WHISKY TRADE, WHO FOUNDED THE MODERN INDUSTRY AS WE KNOW IT

Duncan Forbes of Culloden was one of those distinguished patriots who ardently felt the love of country, and detestation of the cruel tyranny which oppressed Scotland, and took up arms at the time of the revolution and contributed to drive out the family of the persecutors and establish King William on the throne. This was not accomplished without great expense. The resentment of the opposite party against him was intense; and during his absence in Holland they invaded the barony of Ferrintosh, wasted his lands and destroyed the distillery there. As a small compensation for his loss and as a public testimony of his meritorious conduct the government and parliament in 1690 granted to him and his successors, the excise of the lands of Ferrintosh, of the distilleries of all malt produce from the lands, for the annual rate of 400 marks Scots, subject, however, to a similar proportion of any other additional excise which might be imposed on the kingdom. The effect of the excise being thus fixed to a limited sum, for the whole barony, however many might be the distilleries and whatever quantity of spirit they produced, was the cause of the erection of distilleries and the great increase of the business of Ferrintosh and, consequently the increased value of the land to the proprietor, in a two-fold degree, by the encouragement given to the growth of barley and the process of converting it into spirit.

In 1786, the government thought proper to redeem this grant and a sum of £20,000 was given as a compensation, being about sixteen years' purchase, according to what was proved to be its annual value.

"Lord Farintosh", the nickname given to a regular customer at the Cave of Harmony, London, who had drunk five glasses of whisky-and-water every night for many years.

During the ninety-four years in which Ferrintosh enjoyed its privilege, the extension of the trade was great, and Ferrintosh whiskey obtained a reputation which still continues.

JAMES MITCHELL

When a man goes to Caprera, he, as a matter of course, brings a letter of introduction to Garibaldi — when I went to Fort William, I, equally as matter of course, brought a letter of introduction to Long John. This gentleman, the distiller of the place, was the tallest man I ever beheld out of an exhibition — whence his familiar *sobriquet* — and must, in his youth, have been of incomparable physique. The German nation has not yet decided whether Goethe or Schiller is the greater poet — the Highlander has not yet decided whether 'Long John' or 'Talisker' is the finer spirit. I presented my letter and was received with the hospitality and courteous grace so characteristic of the old Gael. He is gone now, the happy-hearted Hercules — gone like one of his own drams! His son distils in his stead — but he must feel that he is treading in the footsteps of a greater man. The machinery is the same, the malt is of quality as fine, but they will never produce whisky like him who is no more.

ALEXANDER SMITH

William Grant
"The Major"

Lord grant guid luck tae a' the Grants,
Likewise eternal bliss,
For they should sit among the sa'nts
That make a dram like this.

WORDS INSCRIBED BELOW A PORTRAIT OF WILLIAM GRANT, FOUNDER OF GLENFIDDICH

Captain William Grant of the Auchorachan Distillery *Glenlivet* begs to acquaint Connoisseurs in whiskey, that in that far-flung Glen, which wholly belongs to the Duke of Richmond, there is no other Distillery than *his own* and that of *George Smith of the Drumin Glenlivet* Distillery — nor within several miles of it and the Public is respectfully cautioned against any other Distillery assuming that title.

NORTH BRITISH ADVERTISER, LATE 1840s

November 6. 1865.

The District of Glenlivet, a part of the Gordon property in Scotland belongs to me. My tenants George and John Gordon Smith, whose distillery of malt Whiskey is called "The Glenlivet" "Distillery" — are the only distillers in the Glenlivet district —

Richmond.

In 1823 an Act of Parliament was passed which made legal distilling a reasonable proposition.

When the new Act was heard of in Glenlivet and in the Highlands of Aberdeenshire they ridiculed the idea that anyone should be found daring enough to start legal distilling in their midst. The proprietors were very anxious to fulfil their pledge to the Government and did everything they could to encourage the commencement of legal distilling; but the desperate character of the smugglers and the violence of their threats deterred anyone for some time. At length in 1824, I, George Smith, who was then a robust young fellow, and not given to be easily 'fleggit', determined to chance it. I was already a tenant of the Duke and received every encouragement from his Grace and his factor Mr Skinner. The outlook was an ugly one, though. I was warned by my civil neighbours that they meant to burn the new distillery to the ground and me in the heart of it. The laird of Aberlour had presented me with a pair of hair trigger pistols worth ten guineas, and they were never out of my belt for years. I got together two or three stout fellows for servants, armed them with pistols and let it be known everywhere that I would fight for my place to the last shot. I had a good character as a man of my word and, through watching by turns every night for years, we contrived to save the distillery from the fate so freely predicted for it. But I often, both at kirk and market had rough times of it among the glen people.

GEORGE SMITH OF UPPER DRUMIN IN GLENLIVET

Distilleries

This book is almost entirely concerned with malts — the single whiskies made in pot stills from malted barley in over one hundred distilleries scattered over the Lowlands, Highlands and Islands. Some of these distilleries are two centuries old — historic, romantic and frequently sited in idyllic rural countryside.

But the bulk of whisky is made from maize and barley in frequently far from romantic industrial complexes in the centre of cities. Grain whisky, as it's called, is produced in continuous stills, and almost the entire output is blended with malt whiskies to produce the 350 brands of Scotch which range from expensive de luxe whiskies containing the finest malts to cut-price loss leaders with remarkably little merit.

All whisky must be aged for a minimum of three years in oak but it is the single malts which command the most attention. Although in their unmarried state they account for only 2.2 per cent of sales, without them there would be no Scotch whisky industry.

When Queen Victoria came to the throne whisky was scarcely drunk outside Scotland. But with the building of Balmoral and the arrival of sporting English aristocrats and industrialists in the Highlands malt whisky was discovered. Ghillies produced it on the river bank; it warmed the tweed-clad stalker on the autumnal moors and the habit was repatriated to London. Many of the wilder malts proved too fiery when removed from their native glens. Experiments were made by mixing gentler malts with the more strongly flavoured to try and produce something more acceptable to the English palate. In 1853 Andrew Usher, an Edinburgh spirit merchant, marketed the first vatted malt — Ushers Old Vatted Glenlivet. It was a success. Other merchants began blending cheaper grain whiskies with malts to cut down costs and produce a

smoother dram. The growth of the railway system helped spread the new blended whiskies to every corner of the country. At almost the same time the vineyards of France were being ravaged by phylloxera and when supplies of cognac became scarce brandy and soda gave way to whisky soda. By the end of the century whisky had become an international success. It was men with names like Haig, Bell, Dewar, Buchanan, Grant and Mackinlay who made the brands that became familiar in every bar from Seattle to Singapore. Without those blends the fine malts would perhaps never have survived and, although the highest art of all is the creation of malts like Macallan, Glenlivet, Glenmorangie, Glenfarclas, Highland Park and Lagavulin, the commercial art of blending is no less essential.

It has been described with precision by the managing director of Macdonald Martin Distilleries as 'the art of combining meticulously selected, mature, high-quality whiskies, each with its own flavour and other characteristics, with such skill that the whole is better than the sum of its parts, so that each makes its own contribution to the finished blend without any one predominating'.

Although there is a growing body of scientific knowledge about the processes of distillation and maturation the good malts can only be made with skill. As Alfred Barnard pointed out a hundred years ago, 'very many persons think they can blend whisky and that it is just a matter of throwing a few brands together. The manipulation of whiskies requires as much care as the most delicate wines.'

The most northerly distillery in Scotland is Scapa, the most southerly is Bladnoch. The smallest is Edradour, the largest Tomatin, the highest is Tomintoul, the lowest is Caol Ila, the most westerly is Bruichladdich, the most easterly is Glenugie. The oldest is probably Glenturret, founded in 1775, the newest Allt a Bhainne built in 1975. The heaviest known distiller was John Smith, a train buff, who in 1869 deliberately sited his distillery of Cragganmore alongside the Strathspey Railway line. Smith weighed 22 stone and because of his enormous girth, although he travelled everywhere by train, was unable to get through the door of an ordinary carriage and was thus forced to travel in the double-doored guards van. The last distillery to be built in the nineteenth century was Glen Elgin (1898); the first to be built in the twentieth century was Tormore (1959). The first blenders to sell their whisky by the bottle were Dewar's. Before Gladstone's Spirit Act was passed in 1860 whisky could only be imported into England in cask. The first firm to bottle Scotch with a screw-top capsule was White Horse; Glenkeith-Glenlivet, built in 1957, was the first distillery to use gas-fired stills.

The distillery was built in the year 1825 by one John Robertson of Crathie, an old smuggler, and it came into the hands of Mr John Begg in the year 1845. It is situated within a mile of Balmoral Castle; there is no distillery within fifty miles around, therefore its isolation gives it a distinctive character. It was first visited by Her Majesty and His Royal Highness the Prince Consort on the 12th September 1848 . . . and we were informed that the whisky made at the distillery has been supplied to the Royal Palaces and Court for the past thirty-six years.

ALFRED BARNARD AT ROYAL LOCHNAGAR

On the morning of our arrival the whole place looked like a busy village, and we were informed that some unusually heavy export orders had arrived, and deliveries by that day's steamer were most important. There was a foreign air about the whole proceedings; the dazzling whiteness of the concreted buildings, the numerous carts, gaily painted a crimson and green colour, laden with casks of whisky, the big coopers with their leathern aprons, the noise of the blacksmiths' anvils, the distillery clerks and excisemen running to and fro, reminded us of the champagne districts. There are 200 workmen employed, for whom the proprietor has provided most comfortable, and, in some cases, most picturesque dwellings.

NEVIS DISTILLERY, FORT WILLIAM

And then I came up to Speyside and there I bided. And that territory included more than the basin of the Spey; it included the Dev'ron, the Fiddich, the Spey, the Lossie, the Findhorn and the Nairn, from Glenlivet — the real Glenlivet — to Inchgower near Buckie, from Glendronach near Huntley, to Brackla at Cawdor. Into that soberly rolling chimney-stalked territory three dozen of us young fellows used to gather for the distilling season from October to May; lads from all Scotland, England, Wales and Ireland, the four most quarrelsome nations in the world — but it was not blood that flowed.

We really were a friendly, easy-going, non-conforming community—distillers, brewers, and revenue alike—and we were extraordinarily continent. Continence is the only way between a palate and malt whisky, and we were as continent as a connoisseur with a vintage claret . . .

But when I do get the first whiff of, say, Standfast, I see a vision. I see the long-winding valley with the chimney stalks and kiln-pagodas above the trees; I see the Fiddich and the Dullan running fast and clear over bright gravel, the bald Convals fringed with a hair of pines, big Ben Rinnes with cap atilt over the glen; I smell again the peat, the wash, and the feints, and feel the tightness of carbon-dioxide in my throat; and I see myself getting out of a warm bed in the dark of a Januar' morning. And I see a girl with red hair.

MAURICE WALSH

This (is) the most remote distillery in the kingdom. It is built in the form of a parallelogram and

enclosed by substantial stone walls. There are three barley store rooms and two others for malt. The kiln is floored with metal plates, and heated in the usual way by a fire, wherein peat only is burned. In close proximity is the mill, containing a pair of metal rollers for crushing the malt. In the mill store, which combines a mash house, are the heatings copper and the mash tun, a vessel 10 feet in diameter and 5 feet deep, with a large tank underneath it, used as an underback. The tun room contains four washbacks, each holding 2,200 gallons, fixed on solid blocks, a wash charger with a capacity of 1,100 gallons and three receivers suitable to the requirements of the above vessels.

The distillery being situated on the side of a hill, no pump is required until the wort is run into the wash still. In the little old-fashioned still house are to be seen two of these 'sma' old Pot Stills', each holding 300 gallons. One of these, a veritable smuggler's still of a peculiar shape, is the quaintest we have seen in our travels, and was formerly the property of a noted law evader; its body is shaped like a pumpkin, and is surmounted by a similarly shaped chamber one-fourth the size to prevent the goods boiling over, through which the neck passes to the head of the still. On the floor of the house is placed an old-fashioned low-wines and feints charger, a stumpy-looking vessel constructed of timber. This building is the oldest part of the work, and consists of a vaulted chamber cut out of the solid rock, and was formerly used by the smugglers as the still and mashing house.

BARNARD AT STROMNESS DISTILLERY, ORKNEY

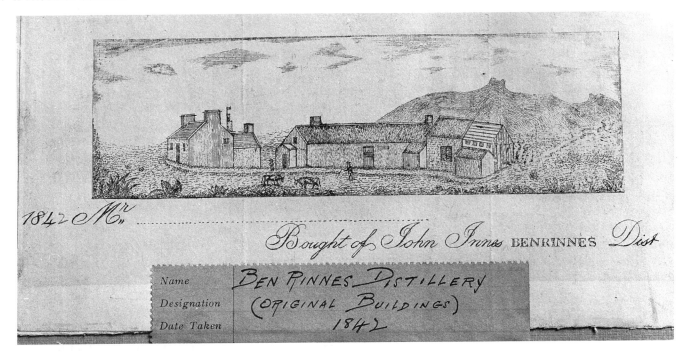

1842 *Mr* ....

Bought of John Innes BENRINNES *Dist*

Name	BEN RINNES DISTILLERY
Designation	(ORIGINAL BUILDINGS)
Date Taken	1842

Our next halting place was Cromdale, and although the Carron Station had been open for more than twenty years, we were the only persons who had ever booked to Cromdale first class, the number of our tickets which were faded with age, commencing at nought . . . We tasted some 1873 whisky and found it prime, and far superior in our opinion to old brandy. Some of this whisky was supplied, by desire, to the proprietor of the Gairloch Hotel, Lochmaree, in 1878, for the special use of her Majesty the Queen, and her suite.

ALFRED BARNARD, VISITING BALMENACH

You can seen Glenfarclas a long way off lying amid moorland at the foot of Ben Rinnes. It was started by Robert Hay, a tenant farmer, in 1836. In 1865 it was acquired from his executors by John Grant for the sum of £511.19s. When I visited the distillery in the autumn of 1982 there was a small cask of whisky standing at the door of one of the warehouses waiting to be collected by its owner. I asked the Excise officer, one of the few women in the service, how much duty had been paid on that particular octave, holding around ten gallons. About £510 she said.

Never was there such a soft, bright landscape of luxuriant green, of clustering foliage, and verdant banks of wild flowers, ferns and grasses. The whole scene is dainty enough for a fairy's palace and we do not wonder at the choice of the ancient Queen, who, during the wars between the Danes and the Scotch, selected Dailuaine as a resting place, and pitched her tents there as she journeyed to join her husband after the battle of Mortlach.

Outside all is quiet and the stillness of death reigns; inside it is all life, bustle and activity and the establishment a little world of industry in itself. In this retired spot, far removed from noisy cities and prying eyes, surrounded by all that is beautiful and lovely in nature, is carried on the mystery of John Barleycorn — his death, burial and resurrection. No wonder with these surroundings that the pure spirit emerging from such an Eden should be appreciated by mortals all the world over.

ALFRED BARNARD, AT DAILUAINE DISTILLERY

Banff was the only distillery to be attacked during the last war. It was closed in 1983 and demolished in 1985.

On the afternoon of Saturday 16 August 1941 a single enemy aircraft came out of the sea-mist and flew low over Banff and the distillery. The malt-barns used as billets by the King's Own Scottish Borderers were machine-gunned, and high explosive bombs were dropped on no. 12 warehouse. Nobody was injured, but the warehouse caught fire and burned to the ground.

Exploding casks of whisky were seen to fly in the air, and others were deliberately smashed to prevent the fire from spreading. It was extinguished before darkness fell, after two fire brigades, helped by the troops, had fought it for many hours. In the words of the local newspapers, 'thousands of gallons of whisky were lost, either by burning or running to waste over the land ... and so overpowering were the results that even farm animals grazing in the neighbourhood became visibly intoxicated'. It is said that ducks and geese dabbling in the Boyndie Burn were recovered on the edge of the sea, and that cows were not milked because they could not be got on their feet.

BRIAN SPILLER, THE DISTILLERS COMPANY LTD

Grandtully is the smallest distillery in the United Kingdom. (It) is all under one roof, and is built on the side of a hill, through which the Cultilloch Burn falls on its way past the farm down to the River Tay, a quarter of a mile distant. It is the most primitive work we have ever seen. The whole 'bag of tricks' could be put inside a barn, and a child four years old could jump across the streamlet which drives the water-wheel and does all the work of the distillery. There are two little stone-built warehouses, containing 200 casks of whisky. We tasted a sample, six years old, and found it delicate in flavour, and smooth to the palate.

ALFRED BARNARD

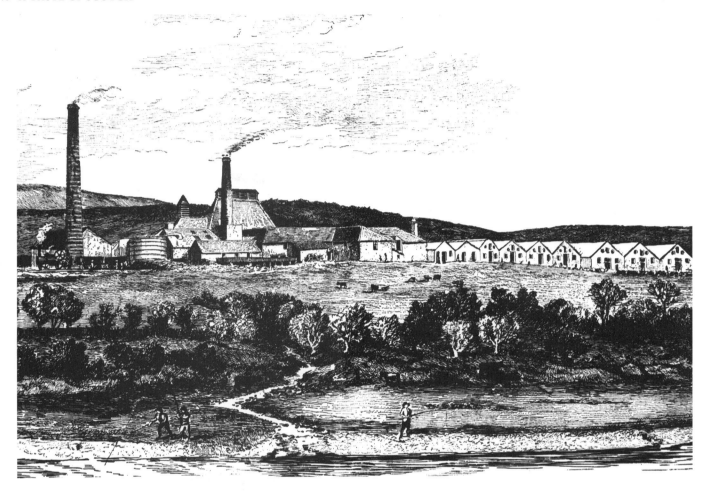

Glenlivet it has castles three
Drumin, Blairfindy and Deskie,
And also one distillery
More famous than the castles three.

ANON

Auchorachan, Upper Drumin and Minmore
Those were the distilleries of yore,
Which made Glenlivet whisky famed,
And ever 'The Glenlivet' named.

TRADITIONAL

It was the practice of the time for the men to receive a large 'dram' once or twice a day, augmented at the slightest excuse by additional drams for performing dirty jobs and sometimes for performing little more than normal duties. The manager appeared to see this practice as being good for morale, whilst most wives and local publicans took a different view. The practice of 'dramming' is now defunct.

DAVID DUNCOMBE, H.M. CUSTOMS & EXCISE

James Allardes, the founder of Glendronach, often dined at Huntly Lodge, and at Gordon Castle when the Marquis succeeded to the Dukedom. On one occasion, he had partaken rather too much of the Glenlivet, and complimented her Grace on her fine playing, paying her other high compliments. Her Grace resented or seemed to resent this, for Mr Allardes was rather a privileged guest. Next morning, however, the Duke told him that the Duchess was much displeased with him last evening. Mr Allardes was very grieved at this, but he managed to get out of the difficulty. 'Well, your Grace, it was just that trash of Glenlivet you gave me yesterday that did not agree wi' me. If it had been my ain gweed Glendronach, I would not have been ony the waur.' The result was that a cask of Glendronach was ordered by His Grace.

BANFFSHIRE JOURNAL, 10 FEBRUARY 1920

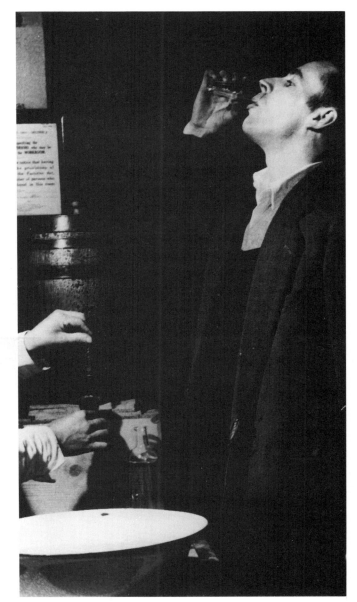

Dramming

On 31 May 1983 the Distillers Company, in a move to 'attain the requisite balance between maturing stocks of whisky and the anticipated level of future sales', closed eleven of their forty-five malt distilleries:

Banff (1863), Benromach (1898), Brora (1823), Dallas Dhu (1898), Glen Albyn (1884), Glenlochy (1898), Glen Mhor (1894), North Port (1820), Knockdhu (1892), Port Ellen (circa 1823) and St Magdalene (circa 1790).

On 31 March 1985, in a move to cut production still further, DCL closed ten more distilleries:

Royal Brackla (1812), Coleburn (1896), Convalmore (1894), Glenesk (1898), Glentauchers (1897), Glenury (1833), Imperial (1897), Mannochmore (1971), Millburn (1876) and Teaninich (1817).

CANAL WHARF, PORT DUNDAS DISTILLERY.

During this period part of Glendullan and Linkwood distilleries ceased production. The malting plant at Port Dundas and Carsebridge grain distillery (1852) were

Knockdhu Distillery, 1898

*closed. Four hundred and seventy staff were made
redundant.*

For the first two years the distillery staff consisted
of William Grant and his sons, who carried on their
education at the same time. When the Supervisor of
Inland Revenue came to pay his first visit, he found
Latin and mathematical text-books lying all over the
distillery. On asking to whom they belonged, he
was told that they were the property of the stillman,
the maltman and the tunroom man. All three were
sons of the founder and, later, the stillman became
Dr Alexander Grant, the maltman Dr George
Grant, while the tunman, Charles Grant, became
owner of Glendronach Distillery. Not unnaturally
the astonished Supervisor reported that it was the
most extraordinary distillery he had ever seen.

SIR ROBERT BRUCE LOCKHART ON GLENFIDDICH

The ten most popular brand name words are:
Auld, Old, Scottish, Clan, Highland, King, Royal,
Scots, Loch and Glen. *Of them all 'Glen' is considered
to have the most magic motivating power and the brands
include:*

*Glen Adam, Glen Allan, Glen Baren, Glen Blair,
Glen Bowie, Glen Burn, Glen Calder, Glen
Catrine, Glen Clova, Glen Coull, Glen Crinan,
Glen Deveron, Glen Dew, Glen Douglas, Glen
Drummond, Glen Eagle, Glen Farg, Glen Finnan,
Glenforres, Glen Garret, Glen Garry, Glen Ghoil,
Glen Glamis, Glen Graeme, Glen Gyle, Glen
Hardy, Glen Ila, Glen Keith, Glen Kindie, Glen
Laggan, Glen Leog, Glen Lily, Glen Lyon, Glen
Mist, Glen Nevis, Glen Niven, Glen Osprey, Glen
Rannoch, Glen Ronald, Glen Rossie, Glen Royal,
Glen Sannox, Glen Shee, Glen Shian, Glen Sloy,
Glen Stag, Glen Stewart, Glen Stuart, Glen Talla,
Glen Tosh, Glen Tulloch, Glenavon, Glenberry,
Glenbrae, Glenburn, Glencastle, Glencoe,
Glencraig, Glencree, Glendamore, Glendarroch,
Glendearg, Glendee, Glendonan, Glendoran,
Glendrostan, Glenfoyle, Glenfyne, Glenisla,
Glenleven, Glenlogie, Glenmark, Glenmillar,
Glenmoray, Glenmorden, Glenmore, Glenmoriston,
Glenordie, Glenrob, Glenrosa, Glen's Eagle,
Glenshire, Glenside, Glentarvie, Glentay,
Glentoshan, Glenview.*

*This does not include the thirty malt distilleries which
incorporate the mystic, magical and romantic word in their
name:*

*Glen Albyn, Glenallachie, Glenburgie, Glencadam,
Glendronach, Glendullan, Glen Elgin, Glenesk,
Glenfarclas, Glenfiddich, Glenfoyle, Glengarioch,
Glenglassaugh, Glengoyne, Glen Grant, Glenkeith,
Glenkinchie, The Glenlivet, Glenlochy, Glenlossie,
Glen Mohr, Glenmorangie, Glen Moray,
Glenrothes, Glen Scotia, Glen Spey, Glentauchers,
Glenturret, Glenugie and Glenury Royal.*

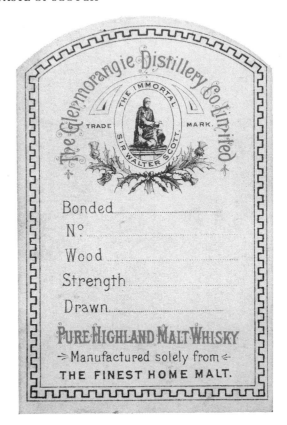

I have drawn the curtain closer,
And from my easy chair
I stretch my hands towards you,
Just to feel that you are there
And your breath is laden with perfume,
As my thoughts around you twine,
And I feel my pulses beating
As your spirit is mingled with mine.

And the woes of the world have vanished
When I've pressed my lips to yours;
And to feel your life-blood flowing
To me is the best of cures.
You have given me inspiration
For many a soulful rhyme —
You're the Finest Old Scotch Whisky
I've had for a long, long time.

TRIBUTE TO SANDY MACNAB'S OLD BLENDED, A
BRAND PRODUCED BY MACNAB DISTILLERIES OF
MONTROSE

We are sitting tonight in the fire glow,
Just you and I alone,
And the flickering light falls softly
On a beauty that's all your own,
It glawms where your round smooth shoulder
From a graceful neck sweeps down;
And I would not exchange your beauty
For the best-dressed belle in town.

The figure of Johnnie Walker in beaver hat, quizzing glass and riding boots was created by an artist called Tom Browne; it was an image that made Johnnie Walker the biggest selling blend in the world.

Some Scots might be offended that White Horse has developed its first new whisky blend for over fifty years specifically for the Japanese market. The Japanese drink their whisky with a lot of ice and water so the blend had to be adapted to 'work' in those conditions. Eleven new blends were produced which were narrowed down to three contenders which were tested and researched in Japan. The resulting blend is White Horse Extra Fine. At the same time the bottle, label and closure were developed and researched, also with an eye on Japanese requirements — not least those of the ladies who run the clubs and drinking places withoutwhich Japanese business would probably grind to a
halt. So it is a dark bottle which does not look ugly when half empty. It has a cork which makes a Cognac-like squeak as you open it, and a striking dark blue label.

HOWARD SHARMAN, *MARKETING WEEK*, 1983

Although Macallan–Glenlivet have been exporting their fine single malt for many years, it was only after considerable thought that it was decided to offer an allocation of the very limited supplies of 1938 and 1950 whiskies to overseas agents. Each agent will receive his consignment complete with hand-written labels to his own specification and in Japan each label will be 'personalized' for individual customers. The cost of a bottle of 1938 in Tokyo will be 150,000 yen.

MACALLAN PR STATEMENT, SEPTEMBER 1980

The Clydeside warehouses of whisky blenders George Ballantine cover 40 acres and hold 25 million gallons of maturing whisky worth £700 million in 1985. The late Tom Scott, Ballantine's managing director, decided that if geese saved Rome from the invading Gauls in 390 BC they might be a perfect security force to alert the two guards to the presence of villains.

Bury the Corkscrew. This is the advice which Messrs. William Teacher and Sons, the well known whisky distillers are tendering to the trade. There is no need at this time of day to draw attention to the difficulty and often danger of drawing a cork by means of a corkscrew. Sometimes the neck of the bottle has come off, resulting in a cut hand, or the cork is rotten and away go the pieces in the liquor. The little device of Messrs. Teacher is simplicity itself. It is in reality a cork stopper with a broad top which is made to fix securely on the mouth of the bottle, and all that one has to do is to give it a twist and hey presto! the cork is out.

LICENSED VICTUALLERS' GAZETTE, JUNE 1913

Name we first the brands that rule in
Islay in the Western seas;
Bruichladdich, Lagavulin,
Bunnahabhainn and Laphroaig.
Once I (lucky fellow!) fell in
With a man who had Port Ellen!
Though, indeed, as good as these
Is Bowmore or Caol Ila,
Celtic witch and arch-beguiler,
Ardbeg, Malt Mill. And I shall
Surely drink more Lochindaal.

Last port seen by westering sail
'Twixt the tempest and the Gael,
Campbeltown in long Kintyre
Mothers there a son of fire,
Deepest-voiced of all the choir.
Solemnly we name this Hector
Of the West, this giant nectar:
Benmore, Scotia, and Rieclachan,
Kinloch, Springside, Hazelburn,
Glenside, Springbank and Lochruan,
Lochhead. Finally, to spurn
Weaklings drunk and cowards sober,
Summon we great Dalintober.

Children of the Highland hills,
Product of the Highland stills,
Now's no hour to ponder faults,
Toy with test-tubes, sniff at malts,
Open-chested must we sing:
Away with care — the drink's the thing!
Fearing neither sir nor madam,
Praise we Dufftown and Glencadam.

Wanderer over hill and moor
Weary, welcomes Edradour,
Purchasing new strength to loin
With Glendronach or Glengoyne,
Glenlochie, or ripe Strath Dee,
Cragganmore and Benachie.
Pious priest at mass or matin
'Mid the murmur of his Latin
Thinks of Mortlach or Tomatin,
Sinning so, but is there any
Sin in dreaming of Balvenie;
Brackla, Millburn or Glenfiddich,
Cardow, Banff, or Teaninich?
Sailor after months of sailing,
Fishing, yachting, cruising, whaling,
Hears the joyous cry of 'land oh!'
Thirsts at once for choice Knockando.
Let the magistracy glower
Let the law put forth its power,
He will drink the good Inchgower,
Tamdhu, Parkmore, Aberlour,
And damnation to the funny

Tribes of ocean in Dalwhinnie —
Drink until the stars go out.
Not for us such deep-sea bout.
Quiet tipplers in our class
Are content with Glenfarclas,
Nor does fancy with us soar
Far beyond sound Convalmore,
Oban, Coleburn or Dalmore,
With mayhap a straying wish
Towards Glen Elgin or Clyne Lish.

Hopeful nephew bound to see
Wealthy and repulsive aunt
(Shadows of a legacy)
Should equip him with Glen Grant,
He will find the interview
Smoother sailing on Knockdhu,
When debate grows overheated,
Chairs thrown down and men unseated,
To restore both law and order
Bring in Dallas Dhu, Glen Cawdor,
Speyburn, Longmorn, or Strathmill.
Quick the tempest will be still
And sweet reason reign again
With the flow of Dailuaine.
If an angel unawares
Your domestic table shares,
You will not be wrong to give it
Tumblers of the real Glenlivet!
Serious poets, short of rhymes
As we all may be at times —
For *ars longa vita brevis* —
Woo the muse with good Ben Nevis,
Though the wench will come no less
For Glengarioch or Stromness,
Scapa or fine Highland Park,
Lighteners of Orcadian dark.
Men will talk most brilliant bosh
On a diet of Ferintosh,
Argue with emphatic oaths,
Black is yellow on Glenrothes,
Prove that four and four make nine
If encouraged by Glenfyne,
And, in paradoxic fury,
Square the circle with Glenurie.

Converts have been made, they say,
To some quite grotesque belief
By Strath Isla and Glenspey
And Glenturret (made in Crieff).
Cunning preachers rope the sullen
Heathen folk in with Glendullan.
In melee or collieshangie
Glentauchers or Glenmorangie
Timid mortals will inspire
With a high heroic ire,

Though their sudden fits of wrath'll
Quickly pass before Blair Atholl.
Leaders of the hopeless charge
Rallying for one assault more,
Should have come equipped with large
Flasks of Pulteney or of Aultmore
Or at least another score
Liquors veterans will think good:
Islay Ben Romach, Glen Mohr,
Balmenach, Glenburgie, Linkwood,
North Port, Angus-reared at Brechin.
Aberfeldy or Ballechin.
While the vanquished in the fray,
Fleeing to the nearest bar,
Counsel take with Auchenblae,
Comfort seek in Lochnagar,
And, when human courage fails,
Stronachie the foe assails.
Scholar, drinking with a lout,
Knocked his boon companion out,
Bawling egotistically, 'Shall an
Imbecile enjoy Macallan?

Craigellachie and Imperial
Are designed for souls aetherial!'
Sad that academic rage
Should pollute my peaceful page;
Class and faction I abhor on
Towiemore or Ord-Glenoran;
Ragged cap and top-hat glossy
Meet as equals on Glenlossie,
Bury hatchets in a hurry
In Glenugie or Glenmoray,
Talisker or Milton-Duff
(Damned be he cries, 'Hold, enough!')
Rounding off at last the story
(Highland section) put we *finis*
With Glen Albyn, Tobermory,
Glenglassaugh, and Benrinnes.

AENEAS MACDONALD, RHYMED GUIDE TO THE
HIGHLAND, ISLAY AND CAMPBELTOWN WHISKIES OF
SCOTLAND

Fhairson had a son
Who married Noah's daughter,
And nearly spoilt ta flood
By trinking up ta water.
Which he would have done—
I, at least, believe it—
Had ta mixture been
Only half Glenlivet

BALLAD OF THE MASSACRE OF MACPHERSON,
W.E. AYTOUN

In July 1882 William Sanderson mixed almost a hundred different blends of malt and grain and let his friends taste them blind. He liked no. 69 — so did they. Vat 69 was born. The slogan they gave it was 'Quality Tells'.

The "Johnnie Walker" experts testing whisky samples with the patent testing dial in the sample room

This grand Whisky has in truth been a revelation to us. It is impossible to tell the precise age of it, the Whiskies of which it is a blend have been so often vatted that every drop of it is thoroughly matured. It has, accordingly, passed through its full development in every stage, and is not only old, but ripe and mellow. Every trace of rawness has passed away; the Whisky is bland and smooth to the taste and distinctly insinuating. VAT 69 is not a cheap Whisky in the ordinary acceptance of the term, but at the same time, we consider the price low in view of the quality. Directly we sampled this Whisky we said to ourselves: 'This is the ideal Whisky so many of our Service readers have long been looking for, and hitherto in vain.' In regard to a Whisky such as this the price is a minor consideration. We give this Whisky with no hesitation the premier place among Scotch Whiskies and we have sampled most of them. VAT 69 is, in our opinion, the finest Whisky sold at the present time, and believing it to be such, we have confidence in recommending it to our readers.

THE WAR OFFICE TIMES AND NAVAL REVIEW,
OCTOBER 1905

As long ago as 1950, when I was teaching at Cornell University, I introduced American friends to Mortlach, available at Macy's in New York, and they took to it with enthusiasm. Perhaps the fact that it was matured in plain oak and was virtually colourless was held to be in its favour. I remember that I was asked to give a talk at the University on Scotch whisky and in the course of my remarks I observed that one of the 'best buys' in pot-still Highland malt whisky was the Mortlach available at Macy's. The next time I went to Macy's to re-stock for myself I was told that they were out of stock. When I expressed astonishment, the assistant said: 'Some damn fool professor at Cornell has been telling all his students to buy it, and we've run out.'

DAVID DAICHES

To change the subject a bit, here is an excerpt from another letter. It is from a whisky distiller:

We regret we are reluctantly compelled to return your cheque as owing to Mr Strachey's failure to fulfil his promise to release barley for distilling in Scotland we dare not take on any new business . . . When you have difficulty in obtaining a drink it will be some consolation for you to know that Mr Strachey has sent 35,000 tons of barley to NEUTRAL Eire for brewing purposes.

People must be feeling very warmed-up when they put that kind of thing into a business letter which, by the look of it, is almost a circular letter.

GEORGE ORWELL, *TRIBUNE*, FEBRUARY 1947

Paying For It

"Small Scotch."

To have your currency taxed is the ultimate indignity but that is what happened in Scotland where for decades whisky was money. As early as 1796 the Rev. David Dunoon, Minister of Killearnan in the Black Isle, noted that for his rural flock 'distilling is almost the only method of converting our victual into cash for the payment of rents and servants; and whisky may be called our staple commodity'.

And then there was the role of whisky in modifying the dire effects of cold. Was it not an act of callous inhumanity to tax so efficacious a staple? In March 1798 John Grant of Balnagowan pleaded from his heart for the sorely oppressed Highlander: 'All that is contended for is that he shall have liberty on moderate terms suited to the poverty of his circumstances to convert the growth of his own soil through his personal industry to the necessary beverage of wholesome spirit, whether diluted with water as grog or taken as a cordial dram to brace sometimes the humid, sometimes the bleak piercing winds of the North.'

It is not fair, however, to believe that down in Westminster they didn't regard North Britain as a special case. For a long time the duty on spirits in Scotland was half what it was in England — and if you look upon whisky as currency that meant a pound north of the border was worth two in England. The temptations to smuggle were hard to resist. So serious had whisky-running become by 1830 that the Excise Board set up a special frontier service of sixty officers who stopped stagecoaches and searched carts on their way south.

When the railway line was built between Edinburgh and Newcastle excise men mingled with the passengers at Carlisle and Berwick stations sniffing out contraband bottles. The anomaly was removed in 1855 when the duty north and south of the border was equalized. It was never, however, rendered acceptable and the Scots have always felt that their national drink was being used, indeed abused, to raise revenue for largely Sassenach purposes. At least one minor war in India was financed in Whitehall by putting a few extra pennies on a gallon of whisky. No blow was more painful than the extra duty of 6d per gallon imposed in 1890 as part of a preposterous scheme to compensate licensees of redundant ale houses. A blow not softened when in 1889 this 'whisky money' was diverted to funding technical and secondary education.

Whisky remains one of the most highly taxed products in the country; currently 75 per cent of the retail price of the average bottle of whisky goes to government coffers. The Scotch Whisky Association is quick to point out the way in which whisky is fiscally victimized compared with other beverages: 7.2 pence per centilitre of pure alcohol for the Englishman's beer compared with 15.19 pence for the equivalent in whisky.

But even with this punitive burden of tax and duty whisky remains remarkably cheap. In 1985 Penguin Books reissued their first five titles. They were originally published in the 1930s at 6d a copy when whisky was 12/6 a bottle. Those five volumes today cost £15. If the whisky industry had decided that it was entitled to a similar rate of inflation a bottle today would cost £75!

It's really high time that something was done
To alter the way the country is run.
They're not doing things in the way that they should.
Och! Just take for instance the price of food.

It's twelve and tanner a bottle,
That's what they're asking today.
It's twelve and tanner a bottle,
It takes all the pleasure away.
Before you can get a wee drappie
You have to spend all that you've got,
Och! How can a fellow be happy
When happiness costs such a lot.

WORDS BY DAVID MACKENZIE, SUNG BY THE GREAT GLASGOW COMEDIAN WILL FYFE

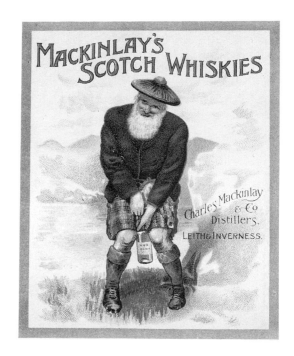

The true Scottish measure is a half-gill or a quarter-gill and such should be demanded. A good innkeeper will serve them. The half-gill is almost double one of the debased English 'doubles'. The English have not only wellnigh emptied Scotland of its native nectar: they have been unconscionable robbers in the retailing of it.

IVOR BROWN

According to the law of Scotland (which is quite a different ass from the law of England) you are not allowed to make water in public or whisky in private!

JACK HOUSE

It is a monstrous injustice that the Banffshire farmer who has toiled at his harvest in the barley-field, the Bansffshire ghillie who has served the shooting-tenant beside the salmon-river or on the moors above the barley, and the Banffshire distillery worker who kindles the peat, dries the grain, and tends the mash-tub and the still beside the river whose water he bewitches with his craft, are all denied the cheap and general enjoyment of the homely miracle they have made.

IVOR BROWN

When David Lloyd George introduced a budget imposing a 33 per cent increase in the tax on whisky, Peter Mackie, purveyor of White Horse, said it was the work of 'a faddist and crank, not a statesman. But what can one expect of a Welsh country solicitor being placed, without any commercial training, as Chancellor of the Exchequer in a large country like this? I might as well bring into my business and place at the head of it a bootmaker or shoemaker or country solicitor and any man will know how incompetent he would be for the job.'

In the whisky trade there was such a distrust of the Welsh Unwizard that it is said that when Sir James Buchanan was buying his peerage, having chosen the title of Woolavington he signed his cheque contributing to Liberal party funds with that name so that it couldn't be cashed until the peerage had been publicly announced.

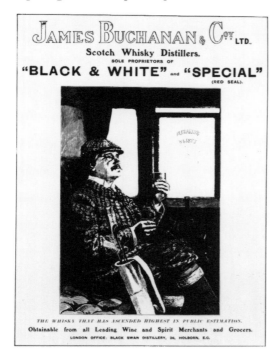

The tax on whisky is manifestly a stupid tax. It appears also to be a malevolent tax. One cannot believe it would continue at its present monstrous figure if distilling were an English industry – or should one call it an art?

ERIC LINKLATER

This is our old native drink made in this land from time immemorial. For untold centuries we had it as our cordial in life, distilled from the barley grown round our doors. In these times, because it was free, it was never abused. That is known. Deceit and abuse and drunkenness came in with the tax, for the folk had to evade the tax because they were poor . . . We do not make this drink to profit by it at the expense of the tax. We do not sell it. Just as Donul does not sell a salmon he takes out of the River. Nor would we even make it thus for our own use if we could afford to buy it. But we cannot buy it. We are too poor. The men who have made the law have taken our own drink from us and have not left us wherewith to buy it. Yet they can buy it, because they are rich. I have the feeling that is not just.

NEIL GUNN

Another recollection of these old days brings back the excise-officers who used to be on the watch at the English frontier to examine the luggage of passengers from the north. One of the surviving relics of Scottish independence was to be found in the inland revenue duties which, as they differed on the two sides of the border until they were equalized in 1855 led to a good deal of smuggling. Whisky was then contraband, and liable to extra duty when taken into England. At that time, this liquor was hardly known south of the Tweed, save to the Scots who imported it from their native country.

SIR ARCHIBALD GEIKIE

The Tasting of It

I had rather a remarkable experience in Edinburgh where my host, a Caithness man, produced a bottle of whisky whose contents were beyond any shadow of doubt over 104 years old. The cork was thickly waxed, and the side of the bottle bore a heavy seal with 'SCRABSTER 1830' stamped clearly in circular form. I thought this seal was also of wax, but on trying it with my knife discovered that it was actually embossed in the glass of the bottle. (So that presumably the bottle was home-made as well as the contents.) The glass was smoke-dark in colour and the bottle stood the least trifle awry, gaining thereby somewhat individuality without loss of dignity. This bottle had been presented to my friend by his mother, to whom it had been given as a wedding gift in 1880.

Whisky is generally believed to mature in wood but not in bottle. Assuming this liquor was bottled immediately after it was made—and the 1830 on the glass would rather imply as much—then here was an occasion for the perfect experiment!

Let it be said at once that the liquor in that bottle was matured to an incredible smoothness. I've never tasted anything quite like it in that respect, yet it had an attractively objectionable flavour, somewhere between rum and tar, to our palates. I suggested that the malt must have been dried over a peat fire into which some ship timber – probably gathered on the Pentland shore – had been introduced. But my host hit on what undoubtedly had happened. In these old days when it was the custom to have a fire on the middle floor with a hole in the roof for a chimney, some specks of the old glistening soot from the rafters had fallen among the malt. Perhaps during

the first few years of maturation this might hardly have been detected – or, again, may have been deliberately aimed at as an illusive part of the whole flavour! – But certainly in this extreme age it was all-pervasive; it had become, indeed, the spirit's very breath.

I do not wish to imply that we made martyrs of ourselves, like the first Discoverer, but the experiment required, amongst other things, considerable talk, during the course of which my host produced a much older heirloom in the shape of a linen tablecloth that had been woven by a lady on her own loom in the same northern district of Caithness from Flaxborough and around her own door. Into one corner of the cloth she had worked her initials in her own golden hair – still as bright in colour as the bridal dream that must so often have glistened behind her young eyes. Lovely eyes; lovely enough, we gravely decided before the evening was over, to make even an anti-highland historian blush!

NEIL GUNN

I have never yet met any blend of all malts or of malt and patent that had the individuality and distinction of the perfect sample of single whisky.

NEIL GUNN

Whisky drinkers often assert that malt may be discriminated from blend. The ability to discriminate plays a part in establishing a social order among whisky drinkers, and, certainly on our unit, confident statements are frequently made by soi–disant experts.

In the first edition of his classic *Design of Experiments* Sir Ronald Fisher described a hypothetical experiment which tested the ability of an aristocratic lady to distinguish between cups of tea that had been poured with the milk before the tea and those that had been poured with the milk after the tea. To settle the issue for whisky we resolved to use an adaptation of Fisher's design.

Eight men, all members of our surgical unit (clinical and research), readily volunteered to take part in the experiment. They were informed that three examples of malt whisky would be chosen to represent three distinct areas of production — that is, Speyside, west coast, and north eastern — and that three popular blends would be used. [Glenfiddich, Springbank, Glenmorangie; Bells, Haig, White Horse]

The data confirm the null hypothesis that, within our unit, malt cannot be distinguished from blended whisky and that experience does not alter powers of discrimination. Regular drinkers were able to detect blends more easily than malts only because of the frequency with which they gave the answer 'blend', though again this was no better than random.

We have analysed the Hedonic scores of the eight subjects as one group, so that at future gatherings no pecuniary disadvantages will occur to our funds; so long as the lights are dimmed and the label is covered we may drink and enjoy our whisky in blissful ignorance.

Although we could not draw any statistical inferences, intuitively we felt that the performance of our subjects was influenced by extraneous factors, such as mood and compliance.

Thus, in conclusion, we certainly agree that 'uisgebeatha' has unique properties steeped in romance and mystique but that the inexpert drinker should choose his whisky to suit his taste (and his pocket) and not his self image.

CAN MALT WHISKY BE DISCRIMINATED FROM BLENDED WHISKY? THE PROOF. A MODIFICATION OF SIR RONALD FISHER'S HYPOTHETICAL TEA TASTING EXPERIMENT. STEPHEN J.D. CHADWICK, FRCS, AND HUGH A.F. DUDLEY, CHM, FRCS.

A Kindred Spirit

Fairntosh whisky was much relished in Scotland; it had a strong flavour of the smoke of the peat with which the malt of which it was made was dried; but this was considered as one of the marks of it being genuine.

ROBERT FORSYTH

I have little patience with the pseudo-poetical attempts to describe the differences in flavour of the various malts. It was once explained to me by a lover of Laphroaig, an Islay malt that rolls on you like a sea haar: 'Scottish whiskies are like an orchestra. The Islay malts are heavy and sombre as 'cellos. Highland malts are violas. Lowland the discursive violin, and grains are like pianos – sometimes *fortissimo*, sometimes *pianissimo*.' But such efforts are futile. You can only know any or all of them by actually drinking them.

HUGH MACDIARMID

I used to endeavour to supply my cask with, and to keep independent jars of, the following: Clyne Lish, Smith's Glenlivet, Glen Grant, Talisker, and one of the Islay brands – Lagavulin, Ardbeg, Caol Isla, etcetera. The picturesquely named 'Long John', otherwise Ben Nevis, is less definite in flavour than any of these, but blends very well. Glendronach, an Aberdeenshire whisky, of which I did not think much forty years ago, improved greatly later; and I used to try both of these in my cask. But I always kept separate supplies of all, and amused myself

with these, alone or variously blended, at intervals. A friend of mine from Oxford days, now dead, held some mixed Clyne Lish and Glenlivet of mine to be the best whisky he had ever drunk.

GEORGE SAINTSBURY

It is not too fanciful to believe that whiskies embody the character of the different regions. Lowland whiskies are mild and equable, like the gentle countryside in which they are made. Islay whiskies have the tang of the sea spray that washes the island. From the desolate highlands come whiskies with a flavour redolent of honey and of the rich peat in which over thousands of years the essence of heather, gorse and pure trees have been compressed.

ANTHONY TROON

In my lifetime the old casks, some of which had been used for maturing spirit for fifty years and more, would be given to the workers as a perk. They would pour in a couple of gallons of boiling water and then roll them up and down Whisky Raw, as the row where the distillery stood was known. After the hot water and steam had circulated round and round the cask any whisky in the wood would have been extracted and they'd wind up with a couple of very good gallons for themselves. It was known as 'grogging the cask', but the practice was made illegal just before the Great War.

REV. HARRY RICKETTS OF FETTERCAIRN

These generous whiskies, with their individual flavours, do recall the world of hills and glens, of raging elements, of shelter, of divine ease. The perfect moment for their reception is after arduous bodily stress – or mental stress, if the body be sound. The essential oils that wind in the glass then uncurl their long fingers in lingering benediction and the nobler works of creation are made manifest. At such a moment, the basest man would bless his enemy. And so, convoluting like the oils, we come back to the conception not of conquering but of civilizing!

NEIL GUNN

It is an invidious as well as difficult task to single out any (whisky) for special recommendation, yet a list of twelve names can be made up which will probably win all but universal acceptance as representing Highland whisky at its most distinguished. It is as follows: Glen Grant, Highland Park, Glenburgie, Cardow, Balmenach, Royal Brackla, Glenlossie, Smith's Glenlivet, Longmorn, Macallan, Linkwood, and – . But the twelfth place I decline to fill, being unable to decide even after prolonged spiritual wrestling and debate, whether Talisker or Clyne Lish should be honoured.

AENEAS MACDONALD

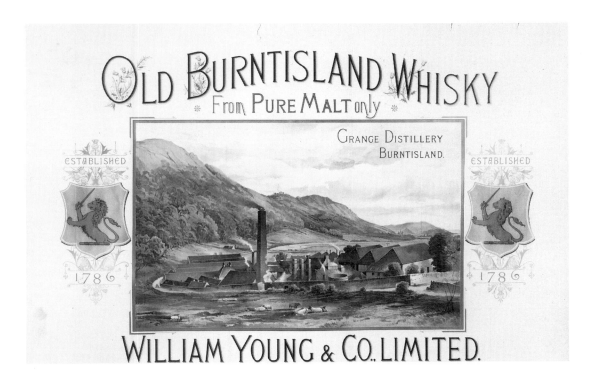

The writer first tasted whisky during an attempt to climb the Cairngorm Range in the late autumn of 1918. The weather was cold; snow was falling and the fingers were so chilled that the packets of sandwiches remained uneaten — it was impossible to untie the strings. The guide broke the ice of the burn, took up a little water in a tin cup and laced it with something from a bottle. The delicious concoction transformed the world. The generous warmth spread to the finger tips and to the frozen toes inside the heavy boots. One realized that to the Highlander whisky was not a luxury but a necessity, a necessity which has been put, alas! increasingly out of his reach by excessive taxation.

JAMES LAVER

I should like to beat the drum a bit for Lowland malts. They have been overshadowed in the literature of whisky and in the esteem of single whisky drinkers by Highland malts, which have more romance in their story and the best of which, it is true, are whiskies of greater character and grander flavour. But a well-matured Lowland malt is — especially for those who do not prefer a heavily-peated whisky — a pleasant and civilized drink of distinctive quality and makes a good all-purpose whisky.

DAVID DAICHES

Leaning against the wind and rain, you drive off from the first tee at Machrie. You feel your ball has gone straight, so with head down you plod on . . . Eighteen holes of that — and then a glass of Lagavulin! It's not that it revives you; it crawls along to your finger-tips and toe- nails in a divine glow . . . But if I had been golfing in a hot sun at Eastbourne — would I have been looking forward to this potent stuff at the end?

AN ENGLISHMAN TALKING TO NEIL GUNN

"Good Judges" drink only John Brown & Co's Scotch Whiskies

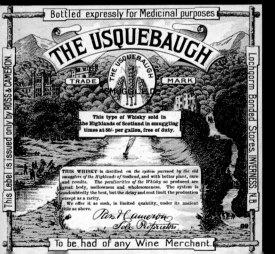

Bottled expressly for Medicinal purposes

THE USQUEBAUGH

TRADE MARK

THE USQUEBAUGH SMUGGLED

This type of Whisky sold in the Highlands of Scotland in smuggling times at 50/- per gallon, free of duty.

THIS WHISKY is distilled on the system pursued by the old smugglers of the Highlands of Scotland, and with better plant and results. The peculiarities of the Whisky so produced are great body, mellowness and wholesomeness. The system is undoubtedly the best, but the delay and cost limit the production except as a rarity.

We offer it as such, in limited quantity, under its ancient title as above.

Ros. & Cameron,
Sole Proprietor.

This Label is issued only by ROSS & CAMERON.

Lochgorm Bonded Stores, INVERNESS, N.B.

To be had of any Wine Merchant.

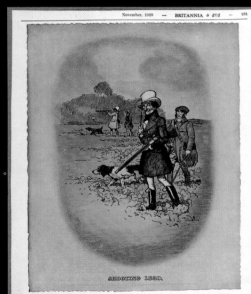

November, 1929 — BRITANNIA & EVE — 181

SHOOTING USED.

JOHNNIE WALKER
Born 1820 —— Still going Strong

SHOOTING: "Up gets a guinea, bang goes a penny, and down (with luck) comes half-a-crown." Values change but the chance remains . . . . . . and the lasting lure of covert and stubble.

JOHN WALKER & SONS, LTD., SCOTCH WHISKY DISTILLERS, KILMARNOCK, SCOTLAND.

Outstanding
in every
characteristic of
High class "Scotch"

"King George IV"
WHISKY

SCOTCH WHISKY
"BLACK & WHITE"

BLACK & WHITE

JAMES BUCHANAN & CO. LTD.   LONDON & GLASGOW

'TIS LOVE THAT MAKES THE WORLD GO ROUND
SO SAY THE LOVERS FRISKY —
BUT IF YE'RE A SCOT, AS LIKE AS NOT
THE WORLD GOES ROUND THROUGH WHISKY!

GEORGE & J.G. SMITH

The
GLENLIVET
12 YEARS OLD

Unblended all malt
Scotch Whisky

Distilled in Scotland by
GEORGE & J. G. SMITH
THE GLENLIVET DISTILLERY · SCOTLAND

Produce of Scotland

OLD BURNTISLAND WHISKY
From PURE MALT only

GRANGE DISTILLERY
BURNTISLAND.

ESTABLISHED   ESTABLISHED
1786   1786

WILLIAM YOUNG & CO. LIMITED.

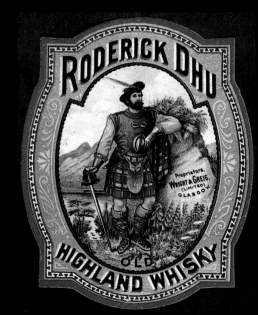

WORTH HUNTING FOR

GILBEY'S
SPEY-ROYAL
WHISKY

DEWAR'S PERTH WHISKY.

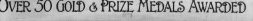

OVER 50 GOLD & PRIZE MEDALS AWARDED

THE CATHKIN BRAES BLEND
SPECIAL OLD
WHISKY.

ESTAB.D 1856.   (REGISTERED)

PROPRIETOR
DAVID W. LECKIE,
WHOLESALE & RETAIL
Wine & Spirit Merchant
63 Washington St., GLASGOW.

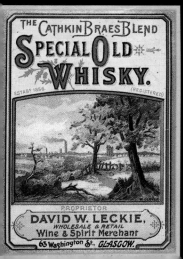

BUCHANAN'S SPECIAL

TRADE   MARK
"RED   SEAL"
FINEST SELECTED OLD SCOTCH WHISKY
AS SUPPLIED TO
THE HOUSE OF COMMONS.

James Buchanan & Co. Ltd.

Distillers, GLASGOW & LONDON.

GLENTAUCHERS-GLENLIVET DISTILLERY, MULBEN, SPEYSIDE. N.B.

THE
"GLEN GRAHAM"

OLD HIGHLAND WHISKY
ROBERT GRAHAM & SONS
GLASGOW

I am offered a sample of the almost colourless liquid. It is spirited enough to power a jet fighter. The pungent, slightly oily, peaty ruggedness of the bouquet mounts into my nostrils. The corpus of the drink advances like the lava of the Cuillins down my throat. Then woom! Steam rises from the temples, a seismic shock rocks the building. My eyes are seen to water, cheeks aflame I steady myself against a chair. Talisker is not a drink, it is an interior explosion, distilled central heating; it depth-charges the parts, bangs doors and slams windows. There's nothing genteel about Talisker.

Talisker at its best can be superb, but I have known it adopt the certain manner of Skye weather. I have two or three pleasant memories of it, however; one in particular, concerning an ex-president of the Alpine Club who used to come to Skye for the Cuillins and fishing. I happened to gather that he had once travelled across Europe to greet a few magnums of a champagne deemed to have been exhausted. We were staying in the same little hotel, where I had happily been presented with a special bottle of Talisker, and I had the very considerable pleasure of watching a meeting between two spirits perfectly matched.

NEIL GUNN

I have tried to procure what a Scotsman would recognize as the best of Scotch whisky. I asked my dear friend Peter Byrne to get his merchant, or should I say in Scotland his factor, to send me a sample of the best of Scotland's produce. He riposted with a bottle of Talisker and I gave it the trial that I think any great produce should enjoy: I drank a little of it as liqueur. And I freely admit that it is a great whisky and I should be sorry to mix it with soda-water or even soft water, for at a sufficient age I think it would make a very good liqueur indeed.

MAURICE HEALY

One of the oldest the oldest recorded whiskies ever drunk was consumed by Joseph Mitchell in the house of Macdonald of Borrodale on the shores of Loch-nan-Uamh. Macdonald's grandfather had sheltered Prince Charles on the first and last nights he spent in Scotland in his quest for the crown. Old Macdonald and all his followers went out with the chief of Clan Ranald to join the Prince in 1745, but before leaving they buried all their plate and valuables and a quantity of whisky in a neighbouring moss. Most of the men died at Culloden. Although the plate was soon discovered, the whisky was not. It was not until 1810 that a keg of whisky was laid bare during the spring peat-cutting. It had been buried for sixty or seventy years and when Mitchell was offered some at Borrodale House in 1838 it was well over ninety years old. It was, said Mitchell, an 'insinuating whisky (which) excited in us the most benevolent feelings during the whole evening'. An even more remarkably whisky was offered me on a winter's morning in 1988 in the Glasgow blending rooms of Lang Brothers. The bottle had been recovered from the Indian Ocean in 1961, part of a consignment of Macallan which had gone down with a ship in 1857, the year of the siege of Lucknow and the Cawnpore massacre. This pre-Mutiny dram, at least 131 years old, was amber in hue, full-bodied and memorably mellow.

Of the other island whiskies, Talisker, the Skye whisky, is the best known. If you breathe the flavour out of your nose immediately after swallowing, you get an after-taste of oily smokiness which I find extremely agreeable. Talisker is not perhaps to everybody's taste, nor is it an all-purpose whisky; but it is a whisky of great character, and certainly the whisky to be drunk in Skye itself when a light rain is falling and the mist is on the hills.

DAVID DAICHES

I must say something of Pulteney – the whisky of my native country – Old Pulteney, as it was always called, though I have childhood memories of seeing it in bottle perfectly white and certainly new. In those days it was potent stuff, consumed I should say, on the quays of Wick more for its effect than its flavour! A very individual whisky, it was naturally disliked by some as ardently as it was praised by others. Whisky has its human parallel. It is not a machine-made article and has to be come upon as one comes upon a friend, and then treated with proper respect. When I got of an age to understand Old Pulteney, I could admire its quality when well matured, recognizing in it some of the strong characteristics of the northern temperament. Though very pronounced in flavour, it was never quite so peaty as some of the Speyside stills, which occasionally err just a trifle in this respect, I think.

NEIL GUNN

Now, when and where do you drink a single malt? First of all, I contend that it should be drunk neat with, if desired, a chaser afterwards. It is a sin to adulterate it with soda, dry ginger or even plain water unless that water is the genuine soft Scottish water from the Highland streams. The best time to drink it is in the evening, after dinner, and as a liqueur, when you have plenty of time to sit back and enjoy it.

JACK MAHONEY

I had an interesting experience with Dalmore in Invergordon just after the war, when I happened to drop into a little 'school' who ordered nine gallons at a time direct from the distillery. Though it was not so old as it might have been, it certainly sustained its reputation; an all-round reliable whisky, capable in its best moods, I should say, of a pronounced excellence.

NEIL GUNN

There is one way to have a whisky that is better than merely good, a whisky that is always uniform, a whisky with merits that can be propagated: and that is to keep a cask. The tap must be about half-way down, so that you know when to refill; thus the goodness of the original spirit is infused into all that you may subsequently add, while the addition gives youthful strength to the body of the old. A friend of mine was given by his father a large sherry cask filled with a great whisky, and for over half a century it has been regularly replenished with spirits as good as he could procure, the result being a drink that no guest of his can fail to remember.

AUGUSTUS MUIR

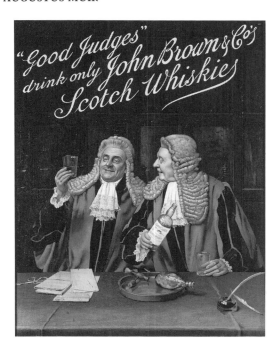

It is strange that there are people who do not like Scotch, but such timid souls do haunt this earth. What they usually dislike is what they describe as a medicinal (or to be pedantic, phenolic) tang. That is the peat. To complain about it is like dismissing a first growth Cabernet from Bordeaux because it has a hint of cedarwood.

A phenolic, peaty nose is found to some extent in most Scotch whiskies, and is one of their defining characteristics, but it is at its boldest in the Islay malts. In that respect they are the most Scottish of whiskies. That is why they are revered by Scotch whisky zealots and why – in tiny proportion, because of their intensity – they are used in almost all blends. Theirs is the character that makes a blended Scotch unmistakably Scottish, and thank heaven for that. It is also the element that frightens drinkers who have a timid palate.

The Islay malts are to whisky what Lapsang Souchong is to tea. The analogy is perfect. During the early months of the summer 'silent season' when the distilleries close for maintenance, some of their workers go peat-cutting on the windswept, boggy, central moorland, starting at daybreak. To refresh themselves, they brew breakfast tea over a peat fire. The tea is rich, sustaining, at once dry and syrupy, perhaps tar-like. It is a Scottish island's earthy counterpart to the Lapsang Souchong of South China. It is the taste of early summer in the season's progress of whisky-making.

MICHAEL JACKSON

FOR AULD LANG SYNE.

One of my pleasanter cellar remembrances is that of dispensing at the doorway a glass of pure Clyne Lish to an oyster-wife who used to supply us with excellent natives at one and ninepence a dozen. 'You won't want any water?' said I, and the lady ejaculated 'Na! Na!' with a smile worthy of Ocean itself.

GEORGE SAINTSBURY

I remember after a long journey I came in the early morning to the house of a Highland author — a man of great charm and noble character — who immediately gave me a glass from which there breathed an aroma no less distinguished and no less happy than that of an ancient brandy. It was flawlessly smooth, of a very grateful and individual flavour, not full-bodied but light-hearted. Nor was it extravagantly old. It was a malt whisky, kept eleven years in wood.

ERIC LINKLATER

France has given claret to the world and the world is better for it. Scotland has it in its power to give to the world such whisky as few can dream of: and the world would again be better. Leoville, Margaux, and Latour might be matched with Islay, Glenfiddich and Glen Grant. Haut Brion, singing aloud, might hear in reply the *voix d'or* of Highland Park. And the brown streams of Glenlivet would need not envy the sun-warmed slopes of Bordeaux. With such whisky to help it the world would grow kindlier and more wise, aware of beauty and comforted with friends.

ERIC LINKLATER

To listen to the silence of five thousands casks of whisky in the twilight of a warehouse while the barley seed is being scattered on surrounding fields, might make even a Poet Laureate dumb. To be a fifteen-year-old butt waiting in a cellar to be removed for bottling, public exhibition, and the foul language of the soda syphon, is perhaps to know the ultimate note in individual tragedy.

NEIL GUNN

After all, my acquaintanceship with Scotch has lasted only a matter of a mere forty-nine years, and you need half-a-century at least to claim some knowledge.

MAURICE WALSH

I have personally sampled a 42-year-old Glen Grant that common sense dictated should not have been allowed to remain in cask for that length of time. But in this case it had worked. It was an astonishing drink; silky and mellow and with harmonies that lingered on the palate for a very long time. I was not allowed very much of it and I was profoundly glad that it had been bottled when it had, and the risks of allowing it another year in cask not taken.

BRIAN MURPHY

Burns as Depute-Master Mason, engraved by Charles Ewart, after Stewart Watson.

Whisky is, of course, a versatile spirit. If fruit, or ice, is added, or sprigs and splashes of this and that — a habit not yet formed by the Scot — what results is not drunk for the sake of these gentle ingredients, but for the golden fellow himself — John Barleycorn. This hero, in the violence of his preparation, is almost a parable of the Scot's own career, and it is the Scot who still sees most deeply into the heart of the noble end-product — whisky. It calls to his nerve ends like bagpipe music. In it he cannot fail to see something of his history, like a beacon-light compressed in a glass. Having long ago sent, broadcast and seen widely accepted his accumulation of social ways and songs and customs it is entirely natural that he should now fit out mankind with the supreme social dram.

SIR ROBERT BRUCE LOCKHART

Burns, the arch-propagandist of the spirit, was an Ayrshire peasant with a peasant's taste for what was fiery and instant. It is probable that the poet laureate of whisky had but the slightest acquaintance with a whisky pleasing to civilized palates and that his muse, as he calls it, was nothing but the abominable Kilbagie of his day. No word of Burns' gives the slightest impression that he had any interest in the mere bouquet or taste of what he drank; on the contrary, his eloquent praise is lavished on the heating, befuddling effects of whisky.

AENEAS MACDONALD

The Drinking of It

BUMFOOZLED!

" THE MAIR I DRINK, THE LESS I'LL HAE !
THE LESS I HAE, THE MAIR I'LL DRINK ! "

'*I don't know why people get so worked up about it,*' a wine-loving friend of mine remarked, '*after all it's only fermented barley put through a still.*' Compared to a fine claret or burgundy it was a sorry thing he said, devoid of complexity, good for a nightcap on a cold night but not much more. And yet whisky has stirred the pens of great men; there must be something about it beyond its mere capacity to warm the veins. It is intoxicating in every sense of the word.

There is an apocryphal story told of an old connoisseur of Scotch called Angus who had spent his working life extolling the virtues of John Barleycorn in various advertising agencies. After a fall down a flight of stairs one night he was received at the portals of heaven. The presiding angel, an awesome figure in toga towelling, inquired how Angus had passed his time on earth.

'In praise,' said Angus.

'In praise of what?' asked the bearded one.

'The water of life your reverence,' said Angus, 'uisge beatha, *the liquid gold distilled from the dew of hill and glen and ben and bannock; wrung from the pages of history since time immemorial.*'

'You allude to a drink?'

'THE drink,' corrected Angus, 'the drink of kings and the king of drinks. A beverage to paean, a thesaurus of potions.'

'And what is this drink made from?'

'Earth and fire and water. Golden barley from the heartlands of Moray, malted by craftsmen, dried over pungent fires fed by peat laid down when dinosaurs roamed the primeval pine forests. Mashed with delicate yeasts and heated in hand-beaten copper stills until the indefinable vapours rise in a symphony of headiness to be gently condensed into ardent liquor.'

'Is this an industry of which you speak?'

'No,' said Angus drawing himself up to his full if slightly bruised stature, 'it is a mystery as old as time itself. Within those bulging and burnished alembics an arcane alchemy occurs which would have confounded Paracelsus, Geber, John of Dee, indeed Faustus himself.'

'And one drinks this liquid?'

'Not at once. Long does it lie in seasoned wood yielding its fiery secrets to the temperate and tempering atmosphere until the marriage of spirit, air and oak gives birth to a distillation so smooth, so matured, that it almost defies description.'

'Almost?'

'Almost, but not quite. Within that amber nectar lies a whole symphony of sensations. A potation as mellow as heather-honey, warm as a thousand Highland welcomes, bold as the skirl of pipes, bracing as the northern wind and as strong as the great breakers that pound the sea cliffs of the Hebrides. It has the taste of peat-brown burns within it, the love and laughter of freckled lassies and the cry of the wild adman on the wing.'

'And its value?'

'How to encompass that in one word? It qualifies the vagaries of climate, rouses flagging energies and stimulates jaded appetites. It is ideal for invalids, those of timid or flatulent disposition and strongly recommended for victims of involutional melancholia. As a specific for flu, marasmus, strabismus, specific aboulia and dizzy spells it is unrivalled. Doctors not only recommend it but drink it in large quantities.'

'It is then a work of art?'

'But of course. It is part of our heritage, too, warp and woof, kith and kin; a timeless and truly noble spirit. A masterpiece of cooperation between man and nature — Hibernia's gift from the gods, a mysterious and romantic elixir. Consider the delicacy of the aroma, the deep mellowness, the wonderful dietetic properties, the absolute purity and stimulating power!'

'And this whisky, is it easy to make?'

'Far from it. The elements of the mystery defy analysis. Even the chemists in their white coats, the gas chromatographers, the urinologists, know not what subtle enigmas occur within the graceful swan-necked stills. Ask not how the crystal granite-cold burn water, the burgeoning barley and the distillers' cunning combine to create this unique flavour and bouquet.'

'Could not a computer be programmed to make whisky?'

'No computer could ever match the skills handed down by generations of reticent and slightly squished Scotsmen.'

'And there are different kinds of whisky?'

'Yes, bless your excellence, of course there are. Some are prosaic, others as thunderous as a mighty organ, rich symphonies of flavour, libraries of complex taste. You have your full-bodied and assertive whiskies and those which are rich, fragrant, robust, virile, fruity, lush, dissembling, mild . . .'

'So it is a catholic drink?'

'Not wishing to give offence,' said Angus cautiously, 'I think I'd rather describe it as a presbyterian drink, sir. Not free presbyterian, the crippling tax takes care of that, but it's still a drink for all seasons, one that suits the occasion as nothing else will do and with nothing but good effect. As much a symbol really as your kilt or your thistle. Renowned in poetry and song, sir, a poem in itself, music in the ears . . .'

'And what does it do for you?' asked the angel.

'Well it makes you drunk for a start.'

'Most interesting.'

The bloodshot eye of Angus brightens. 'Do I qualify then for entry, do I get a harp and wings?'

'You know of course we are teetotal up here. Strictly hallelujahs, rejoicing, that sort of thing.'

But Angus was already descending the stairs seeking more kindred and eternal spirits below.

"Say WHEN, Man!!"

On Deeside there flourished a certain Saunders Paul (whom I remember an old man), an innkeeper at Banchory. He was said to have drunk whisky, glass for glass, to the claret of Mr Maule and the Laird of Skene for a whole evening; and in those days there was a traditional story of his despatching, at one sitting, in company with a character celebrated for conviviality – one of the men employed to float rafts of timber down the Dee – three dozen of porter. His friend and porter companion was drowned in the Dee, and when told that the body had been found down the stream below Crathes, he coolly remarked, 'I am surprised at that, for I never kenn'd him pass the inn before without comin' in for a glass.'

DEAN RAMSAY

When the cloth was drawn, and the never-failing salver of quaichs introduced, John of Skye, upon some well-known signal, entered the room but *en militaire*, without removing his bonnet, and taking his station behind the landlord, received from his hand the largest of the Celtic bickers brimful of Glenlivet. The man saluted the company in his own dialect, tipped off the contents (probably a quarter of an English pint of raw *aqua vitae*) at a gulp, wheeled about as if the whole ceremony had been a movement on parade, and forthwith recommenced his pibrochs and gatherings.

JOHN GIBSON LOCKHART,
THE LIFE OF SIR WALTER SCOTT

A whisky bottle's an awfu' inconvenient thing; its owr muckle for ane, an' nae eneuch for twa!

OLD HIGHLAND LAMENT

One whisky is all right; two is too much; three is too few.

EVEN OLDER HIGHLAND LAMENT

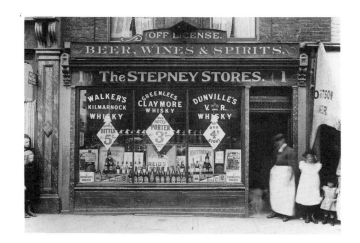

Ale was the favourite beverage during dinner, but there was plenty of port and sherry for those whose stomachs they suited. The quaichs of Glenlivet were filled brimful, and tossed off as if they held water.

J. G. LOCKHART, THE DINNER OF THE ABBOTSFORD HUNT

The first time I visited Cognac, many years ago, I was surprised and amused to find my hosts, distinguished distillers and blenders of brandy, taking Scotch-and-soda before dinner while their English guests politely took the cognac of the house with water—*fine à l'eau*. That was *le snobisme of the time*.

CYRIL RAY

I knew of Highland families in which whisky was as naturally in the home as milk. It was consumed as a normal Englishman will consume a glass of beer—when he needs it, with food (a dram *before* food, for the gael. Our fashionable cocktail had at least a decent ancestor), or for convivial occasion. Even lads of school age would get a drop of whisky when they physically needed it. And *I* have never known in my own experience—or learned from another—of any such lad ever becoming in afterlife a drunkard. To abuse so natural a gift of the life-giving barley would have been looked upon as a weakness akin to some curious form of moral decrepitude. But such drinks as wines and brandies, they were new and exciting as would have been ladies with painted eyebrows; they were disturbances from beyond the home, they stood for the romantic outside world, for licence and debauch.

NEIL GUNN

None of the Teacher dram shops was used in the manner of a modern pub. A customer laid his money on the counter, a dram of whisky was poured into a thick glass, and the customer, having drained it, went his way. Treating was not allowed, and for this reason William and his sons on one occasion were congratulated by the licensing magistrates on being temperance reformers!

William Teacher also forbade smoking, and, in addition, to prevent over-drinking on his premises, ensured that none of his whisky should add to the befuddled state of a man already the worse for liquor. Any would-be customer who had imbibed too freely elsewhere knew better than to enter a Teacher shop. He would have been most unwelcome and the man behind the bar, usually a brawny Highlander speaking sparsely but to the point, would tell him so in emphatic terms.

GEOFFREY E. COUSINS

The great whisky drinkers in my time had their own special way of tasting the stuff. They'd take a dram of whisky first and then some water and shoogle the mixture around in their mouth!

NED SHAW, MANAGER OF INCHGOWER, QUOTED BY JACK HOUSE

Moderation, sir, aye moderation is my rule. Nine or ten is reasonable refreshment, but aifter that it's apt to degenerate intae drinkin'.

OVERHEARD IN AN ANGUS TAVERN

To be fou', or, as he would put it, to have a drappie in his eye, is the Scotchman's notion of bigness and freedom and manly independence. He is a ranter and roarer in his cups, and on the whole much more distressing to meet drunk than sober — which is saying a great deal.

T. W. H. CROSLAND

HERE LIES THE BANES OF TAM MESSER
OF TARRY WOO' HE WAS A DRESSER
HE HAD SOME FAULTS & MONY MERITS
AND DIED OF DRINKING ARDENT SPIRITS
BURNS

Here lie the banes o' Tammy Messer
Of Tarry wood, he was a dresser;
He had some fau'ts and mony merits,
And died o' drinking ardent spirits.

INSCRIPTION ON A HEADSTONE IN A DUNDEE GRAVEYARD

Among curling circles there is a current anecdote of a well known adept at the 'roaring play' who used to be distinguished by a remarkable fur cap which covered not only his head but his ears. Appearing one day without this conspicuous headgear, he was at once questioned by his friends as to the cause of its disappearance. 'Ay,' said he sadly, 'ye'll never see that cap again; it's been the cause o' a dreadfu' accident.'

'Accident!' exclaimed they; 'where? how? have you been hurt?'

'Weel, I'll no' just say I've been hurtit. But, ye see, the laird o' Dumbreck, they tell me, was ahint me, and he was offerin' me a glass of whisky – and I never heard him!'

SIR ARCHIBALD GEIKIE

The different effects of whisky and ale upon the soldiers of the militia regiments have frequently been observed. Whisky produces anger with intoxication but ale generally good humour. Happy would it be if these manufacturers of public poison be everywhere checked and breweries of wholesome ale encouraged in their room.

SIR JOHN CARR

Campbelton is chiefly remarkable for the amazing fact that it is the means of annually contributing *more than one million sterling* to the Inland Revenue in the form of whisky duty. That is to say, the distilleries of Campbelton and its immediate neighbourhood collectively produce upwards of 2,657,000 gallons per annum and whisky-duty is ten shillings per gallon. What a field for the beneficent Blue Ribbon Army, and how justly might they plead that this vast amount of barley should go to feed the thousands, now on the verge of starvation throughout our own North-West!

C. F. GORDON CUMMING

Nothing particular in Court except the account which a worthy sempstress of Campbeltown, a witness gave of her habits. For about twenty-five years she has scarcely ever been in bed after five. The first thing she does after dressing is to go to a rock about a mile off and to take a large draught of water. She then proceeds about another mile in a different direction where she washes the taste of this out by a large draught of fresh water, after which she proceeds home and about half-past six puts on the tea kettle and breakfasts. This is a healthy and romantic seeming morning. And therefore I regret to add that it was proved that three or four times a week the rest of the day is given to whisky.

LORD COCKBURN 1838

IN "GENERAL" USE.

A Commanding Spirit finds its way to the front. PATTISONS' WHISKY commends success because it has been found by the public to be a genuine, wholesome, palatable beverage, carefully blended and thoroughly matured. It is cream-like in taste, with all the stimulating qualities of the pure Highland spirit. Sold Here, There, and Everywhere.

Sole Proprietors: PATTISONS, Ltd., Highland Distillers, BALLINDALLOCH, LEITH, and LONDON.
Head Offices: CONSTITUTION STREET, LEITH.

John Kelly was M'Ian's principal shepherd—a swarthy fellow, of Irish descent, I fancy, and of infinite wind, endurance, and capacity of drinking whisky. In the absorption of whisky he was without peer in my experience, although I have in my time encountered some rather distinguished practitioners in that art. If you gave John a glass of spirits, there was a flash, and it was gone. For a wager I once beheld him drink a bottle of whisky in ten minutes. He drank it in cupfuls, saying never a word. When it was finished, he wrapt himself in his plaid, went out with his dog, and slept all night on the hillside. I suppose a natural instinct told him that the night air would decompose the alcohol for him.

ALEXANDER SMITH

Mackenzie was once at a festival at Kilvarock Castle, towards the close of which the exhausted topers sank gradually back and down on their chairs till little of them was seen above the table except their noses, and at last they disappeared altogether and fell on the floor. Those who were too far gone to rise lay still from necessity; while those who, like the Man of Feeling, were glad of a pretence for escaping fell into a doze from policy. While Mackenzie was in this state he was alarmed by feeling a hand working about his throat, and called out. A voice answered 'Dinna be feared, sir, it's me.'
'And who are you?'
'A'm the lad that louses the craavats.'

LORD COCKBURN

So far as I know, the first name to be recorded in connection with a 'whisky drunk' was Darnley: he had sat drinking with a Frenchman who had not realized the potency of the Scots liquor. It was in later times that we hear of the habit of deep potations, as at the Nine Tumblers Club of St Andrews, where each member was expected of an evening to polish off no less than nine tumblers of toddy and be able to enunciate clearly at the end of it the words '*Bib-lic-al Crit-ic-ism*'.

AUGUSTUS MUIR

Strong drink to the body can do no good;
It defiles the blood, likewise the food,
And causes the drunkard with pain to groan,
Because it extracts the marrow from the bone.

The more's the pity, I must say,
That so many men and women are by it led
  astray,
And decoyed from the paths of virtue and led on
  to vice
By drinking too much alcohol and acting unwise.

A TRIBUTE TO MR MURPHY AND THE BLUE RIBBON ARMY, WILLIAM MCGONAGALL, POET AND TRAGEDIAN

'Depend upon it,' said Mr M, 'it's a bad thing whisky.'
'Weel, weel, sir,' replied Donald, 'I'll not say but it *may*,' adding in a very decided tone – 'speeciallie *baad* whisky!'

DEAN RAMSAY

If the drinking habits of the people had been proportioned to the eagerness with which persons of the middle and lower ranks aided in the production and distribution of contraband liquor, the nation must have become utterly besotted. To defeat or aid in defeating the officers of excise was deemed an enterprise positively laudable. In order to this end, no strategem, however revolting, was deemed offensive or unworthy. Thus at the commencement of the present century, one of the principal hotel-keepers at Stirling, when he required a further supply of whisky, sent a funeral cortège into the highlands of Perthshire, which returned laden, hearse included, with casks of the contraband liquor. To lowland vendors, whose dealings were more circumscribed, women conveyed the illicit product of the mountain-still in a species of panniers, composed of tin, which were constructed so as to rest under the dress in the manner of the modern bustle. Some of those whisky panniers were used in the vicinity of Callander within the last sixty years.

REV. CHARLES ROGERS

O Muse, be kind, and dinna fash us,
To flee awa' beyont Parnassus,
Nor seek for Helicon to wash us,
That heath'nish spring;
Wi' Highland whisky scour our hawses
And gar us sing.

ROBERT FERGUSON

MP Lowries Cooperage. 1887

My father could never have drunk whisky except when shooting on a moor or in some very dull chilly place. He lived in the age of brandy and soda.

WINSTON CHURCHILL

On no account reduce the barley for whisky. This takes years to mature and is an invaluable export and dollar producer. Having regard to all our other difficulties about exports, it would be most improvident not to preserve this characteristic British element of ascendancy.

WINSTON CHURCHILL, MINUTE TO MINISTRY OF FOOD, 1945

To someone of 28, the House seemed full of Titans. Winston Churchill, locked into silence by the hardness of his cerebral arteries, never spoke, but sat broodingly in his place, a wheelchair awaiting his departure in the Members' Lobby. After questions he would be taken to the Smoking Room where he would sit while the Whips drummed up Members to come and sit with him. Greatly alarmed, I was pressed into service. I asked him whether he would like a cup of tea. He fixed me with a watery, pale blue eye and replied, 'No, you bloody fool, a double whisky.' I happily obliged.

JULIAN CRITCHLEY

Sir, As my son Dugal will tell you eef you cannot reid my rite Lachie McFadyen, the fox hunter, will be here to hunt my hill tomorrow night with his dogs. As you said you would like to see a good hunt I let you know as soon as pocbel. Tell Doogal if you will come.

P.S. Bring your gun. A bottle of whiskey would be verra goot, and two was better than wan.

LETTER FROM A KEEPER TO A VISITING SPORTSMAN, QUOTED BY RONALD EDEN

I am very glad the whisky came safe; do not stint so laudable an admiration for the liquor of Caledonia, for I have plenty of right good and young Highland Ferintosh, and I can always find an opportunity of sending you up a bottle.

SIR WALTER SCOTT, WRITING FROM EDINBURGH ON 10 DECEMBER 1813 TO JOANNA BAILLIE, THE DRAMATIST AND POETESS, IN HAMPSTEAD

Inspiring bold John Barleycorn!
What dangers thous canst make us scorn!
Wi tipenny, we fear nae evil!
Wi usquebae, we'll face the devil!

ROBERT BURNS

The whole man, body and soul, like sweet bells jangled, out of tune, and harsh, is fagged with work, eaten up of impatience, and haunted with visions of vacation. At last it comes, the 1st of August, and then—like an arrow from a Tartar's bow, like a bird from its cage, like a lover to his mistress—one is off; and before the wild scarlets of sunset die on the northern sea, one is in the silence of the hills, those eternal sun-dials that tell the hours to the shepherd, and in one's nostrils is the smell of peat-reek, and in one's throat the flavour of usquebaugh.

ALEXANDER SMITH

There, pass it round with wishes for success, and do not 'spill the good creature', for on such a morning as this, believe me, it is most salubrious; manifold indeed are its virtues. What trades does it not quicken? It is a good carpenter, a good mason, a good road-maker, and a most capital deer-driver, provided it be moderately and discreetly dealt with, just as you deal with it, gentlemen.

WILLIAM SCROPE

What is it gives me the necessary sagacity to outwit the inspector? Whisky. What is it that helps me to know just where to put down the net in Loch Sleeport for Waggett's sea-trout? Whisky. What makes me a good shot at the grouse or a snipe? Whisky. What is it makes Maclaren such a hell of a good doctor? Whisky. Love makes the world go round? Not at all. Whisky makes it go round twice as fast . . .

SIR COMPTON MACKENZIE

Whisky belongs to the alchemist's den and to the long nights shot with cold, flickering beams; it is a compact of Druid spells and Sabbaths (of the witches and the Calvinists); its graces are not shameless, Latin, and abundant, but have a sovereign austerity, whether the desert's or the north wind's; there are flavours in it, insinuating and remote, from mountain torrents and the scanty soil on moorland rocks and the slanting, rare sun-shafts.

AENEAS MACDONALD

Whisky is a re-incarnation; it is made by a sublimation of coarse and heavy barley malt; the spirit leaves that earthly body, disappears, and by a lovely metempsychosis returns to the world in the form of a liquid exquisitely pure and impersonal. And thence whisky acquires that lightness and power which is so dangerous to the unwary, so delightful to those who use it with reverence and propriety.

AENEAS MACDONALD

I should be deficient in gratitude to worthy Sir John Barleycorn if I had not bestowed a few words on him who has smoothed the rude path over the mountains, and levelled the boisterous waves of the Western Ocean.

JOHN MACCULLOCH

The dram of whisky does more than 'refocillate' (John Aubrey's word for warning up the inner hearth). It unties a slow tongue. It reassures the apprehensive. But, far more than that, it adds ease to discourse, quickens wit, and gives substance to meditation.

IVOR BROWN

A cogie o yill*
And a pickle aitmeal
And a denty wee drappie o' whisky,
Was our forefathers' dose
For two sweel doun their brose,
And keep them aye cheery and frisky.
Then hey for the whisky and hey for the meal,
And hey for the cogie and hey for the yill!
Gin ye steer a' the gither they'll do unco' weel,
To keep a chiel cheery and brisk aye.

A COGIE O YILL, ANDREW SHERRIF (1762–1800)

* cogie – cup; yill – ale

With the Scots it was whisky or perish. And how
they have survived!

LAWTON MACKALL

When neebors anger at a plea,
An' just as wud as wud can be,
How easy can the barley-bree
Cement the quarrel!
It's ay the cheapest lawyer's fee
To taste the barrel.

ROBERT BURNS

Let other poets raise a fracas
Bout vines, and wines, and drunken Bacchus,
And crabbit names and stories wrack us,
And grate our lug.
I sing the juice Scotch bear* can mak' us
In glass or jug

ROBERT BURNS
* bere or barley

As a friend, whisky has virtues unequalled by any
other form of alcohol. As an enemy there is
no Scot who does not know its dangers and almost
no Scottish family without its whisky skeletons.
They rattle in my own cupboard and I myself have
been near enough to destruction to respect whisky,
to fear it, and to continue to drink it.

SIR ROBERT BRUCE LOCKHART

Scotch whisky to a Scotchman is an innocent as
milk is to the rest of the human race.

MARK TWAIN

'We'll tak' a cup o' kindness yet' (*Robert Burns*, Auld Lang Syne)

Whisky and the Traveller

I made a memorable night-journey from Inverness to Aberdeen on the northern 'Defiance'. It was the last professional trip of a popular guard. At every stage, friends already 'well on', were sitting up to give him a 'send off'; jovial allies scrambled on to the roof to convoy him to the next stage; raw whisky and hot toddy flowed like burn water; the night owls were roused with song and catch; and when I was dropped in the morning at Inverury, the 'Defiance', usually regulated like clockwork, was a full hour behind her time.

ALEXANDER INNES SHAND

The distillation of whisky presents an irresistible temptation to the poorer classes, as the boll of barley, which costs thirty shillings, produces by this process between five and six guineas. This distillation had a most ruinous effect in increasing the scarcity of grain last year, particularly in Isla and Tiree where the people subsisted chiefly on fish and potatoes.

JOHN LEYDEN

Our driver in order to elevate his spirits before setting out on the dreary road had applied himself to whisky, the universal medicine of the Highlanders, and not being extremely accurate in his calculations had raised them considerably over par, and therefore amused himself by dismounting every gate which he encountered and hurling them over the braes or into Loch Etive.

JOHN LEYDEN

Tourist: (to local weather expert)
Well Jock, how's the glass this morning?
Jock: Empty, Sir. SO FAR!

Strangers are often astonished at the extent of the draughts of undiluted whisky which Highlanders can swallow, without any apparent ill-effects. Burt tells us that in his time, that is in the third decade of the eighteenth century, Highland gentlemen could take 'even three or four quarts at a sitting, and that in general the people that can pay the purchase, drink it without moderation'. In the year 1860, in a walk from Kinlochewe through the mountains to Ullapool, I took with me as a guide an old shepherd who had lived there all his life. The distance, as I wished to go, amounted to thirty miles, mostly of rough, trackless ground, and among the refreshments for the journey a bottle of whisky was included. Not being used to the liquor, I hardly tasted it all day, but when we reached the ferry opposite Ullapool, Simon pitched the empty bottle into the loch. He had practically drunk the whole of its contents, and was as cool and collected as when we started in the morning.

SIR ARCHIBALD GEIKIE

In all the wilds I ever visited, I never yet entered the blackest hut without having what was to be given, the best place by the fire, the milk-tub, the oat-cake, the potatoes, the eggs if it was possible to persuade the hens to do such a deed, and a glass of whisky if it was to be found.

JOHN MACCULLOCH

Should a deer-stalker pamper the inner man? Shades of Abernethy forbid! He should go forth lank and lean like a greyhound; the most that can be permitted him is a few cups of coffee, a moderate allowance of fine flowery pekoe, some venison pasty, mutton chops, a broiled grouse, hot rolls, dry toast and household bread, with a few grapes to cool him. Peaches and nectarines may be put in his pocket, because, as he will be sure to sit upon them, they will do him no earthly harm but rather confer a benefit by moistening the outward man. The best part of a bottle of champagne may be allowed at dinner: this is not only venial, but salutary. A few tumblers of brandy and soda-water are greatly to be commended, for they are cooling. Whisky is an absolute necessary, and does not come under the name of intemperance, but rather, as Dogberry says, or ought to say, 'it comes by nature'.

WILLIAM SCROPE

We got at night to Inveraray, where we found an excellent inn. We supped well; and after supper, Dr Johnson, whom I had not seen taste any fermented liquor during all our travels, called for a gill of whisky. 'Come (said he) let me know what it is that makes a Scotchman happy!' He drank it all but a drop, which I begged leave to pour into my glass that I might say we had drunk whisky together. I proposed Mrs Thrale should be our toast. He would not have *her* drank in whisky, but rather some insular lady; so we drank, I think, Miss Macpherson.

JAMES BOSWELL

We ordered tea when we reached the inn, and desired the girl to light us a fire; she replied, 'I dinna ken whether she'll gie fire', meaning her mistress. We told her we did not wish her mistress to give fire, we only desired her to let *her* make it, and we would pay for it. I had seen the landlady before we went out, for, as had been usual in all the country inns, there was a demur respecting beds, notwithstanding the house was empty, and there were at least half-a-dozen spare beds. Her countenance corresponded with the unkindness of denying us a fire on a cold night, for she was the most cruel and hateful-looking woman I ever saw. She was overgrown with fat, and was sitting with her feet and legs in a tub of water for the dropsy — probably brought on by whisky-drinking.

DOROTHY WORDSWORTH

QUANTITY, NOT QUALITY.

English Angler, having discovered there are two sorts of Whisky at the Inn (best at 6d., second best at 3d.), orders a glass each of the Sixpenny.

Gillie (in a whisper to the Maid as she passes). "Make mine twa o' the Threepenny!"

When they met in the morning they were supposed to have breakfasted at home, and perhaps had had their private dram, it being cold work in a dark wintry dawn, to start over the moor for a walk of some miles to end in standing up to the knees in water; yet on collecting, whisky was always handed round; a lad with a small cask—a quarter anker—on his back, and a horn cup in his hand that held a gill, appeared three times a day among them. They all took their 'morning' raw, undiluted and without accompaniment, so they did the gill at parting when the work was done; but the noontide dram was part of a meal. There was a twenty minutes' rest from labour, and a bannock and a bit of cheese taken out of every pocket to be eaten leisurely with the whisky. When we were there the horn cup was offered first to us, and each of us took a sip to the health of our friends around us, who all stood up. Sometimes a floater's wife or bairn would come with a message; such messenger was always offered whisky. Aunt Mary had a story that one day a woman with a child in her arms, and another bit thing at her knee, came up among them; the horn cup was duly handed to her, she took a 'gey guid drap' herself, and then gave a little to each of the babies. 'My goodness, child,' said my mother to the wee thing that was trotting by its mother's side, 'doesn't it *bite* you?'

'Ay, but I like the bite,' replied the creature.

ELIZABETH GRANT OF ROTHIEMURCHUS (1797–1885)

It was nearly midnight before we arrived at Oban and every apartment of the small inn occupied by tourists. We contrived notwithstanding, to obtain three miserable beds in one room, and after our fatigues slept soundly.

Before sitting down to breakfast a footman handed round a glass of mountain dew to the individuals of both sexes assembled, and no one declined the offer. Indeed I presume that the moistness of the climate requires this antidote, and no love of intemperance need be inferred from this its moderate but diurnal use at the same hour.

EIGHTEENTH CENTURY TRAVELLER

Happily I started on the best of all foundations, a capital breakfast. Attend and envy me: *item* first, a steak of broiled salmon; *item* second, a helping from a pie composed of jellied sheep's head, nice, seasoned and palatable; *item* third, a savoury omelet piping hot; *item* fourth, one half of a rizzard haddock; add to these home-baked bread in the form of scones and oatcakes, as well as honey, marmalade at discretion, plenty of cream and real good coffee, and you will give me credit for having breakfasted. There was a dram after, but that is never counted, although the whisky is well disguised in several tablespoonsful of heather honey. We started for the seat of war about seven o'clock mounted on ponies.

J. G. BERTRAM, A VICTORIAN STALKING BREAKFAST

Canongate Tolbooth [A.D. 1591]

Even in Edinburgh, the same spirit runs through the common people; who are infinitely more civil, humanized, and hospitable, than any I ever met with. Every one is ready to serve and assist a stranger; they shew the greatest respect to a person superior to them; and you never receive an impertinent answer. But, after all this, I wish I could say they were more happy: notwithstanding these many excellencies, I find lying, treachery, dissimulation, envy, detraction, and vice, have their respective significations. As to their country, it is beautiful, and grand to a miracle, and, though far from being temperate, is so healthy, that you hear of fewer disorders than amongst any other people; and I declare, in every part that I have been, I never saw either an exceedingly deformed person, or an aged, toothless paralytic highlander. They eat a great quantity of fish dried in the sun, and a cake made of oatmeal, baked hard and flat. Their constant liquor is whisky; which is also made from oats, has a quick taste, extremely heady, but comfortable to the stomach; unpalatable to strangers, though hot and nourishing to those that are used to it.

EDWARD TOPHAM

With the better class of inn in small towns or big villages, I established frequent and friendly relations. In many of them the simple old Scottish cookery was to be had in perfection. In soups they excelled and in light and simple sweets. In many of these inns the venerable waiter, profoundly interested in the prosperity of the house, was an institution. No one of them ever tempted me into trying their wines, but Glenlivet or Talisker was always forthcoming according to the latitudes; or at the worst, the more potent spirit from illicit stills, strong of the peat-reek, though mellowed by age.

ALEXANDER INNES SHAND

In a few moments the eldest daughter of the house entered bearing a tray laden with bottles and glasses which she brought up to my bedside, in order that, as she said, I might 'taste something before I got up'. Not being used to such a matutinal habit, I declined her offer with my best thanks. But she grew quite serious over my refusal, assuring me that my tasting would give me an appetite. In vain I maintained that at breakfast time she would see that I stood in no need of any help of that kind. She only the more ran over the choice of good appetizing things she had brought me. 'Some whusky nate? some whusky and wahtter? some whusky and milk? some acetates?' This last I conjectured to be a decoction of bitter roots in whisky, often to be found on Highland sideboards in the morning. Seeing that a persistent refusal would have displeased her, I consented at last to have some milk and whisky but I did not discover that the draught in any way improved my breakfast.

SIR ARCHIBALD GEIKIE STAYING WITH JESSIE NICOLSON OF LONFERN IN THE ISLE OF SKYE WHILE ON A GEOLOGICAL FIELD TRIP

One kit of boiled eggs; a second, full of butter; a third, full of cream; an entire cheese made from goat's milk; a large earthen pot, full of honey; the best part of a ham; a cold venison pasty; a bushel of oatmeal, made into thin cakes and bannocks; with a small wheaten loaf in the middle, for the strangers; a stone bottle of whisky.

TOBIAS SMOLLETT, *A HIGHLAND BREAKFAST*

Gillespie and Grant were in high spirits next morning at Breakfast. They were so eager to tell me the result of their four-mile tramp to Sunart that it was not easy to sort out the copious details. A man called Angus had acted as their guide and had taken them up to a lonely croft high above Salen Bay. There, a friend of his called John had welcomed them. It had required a good deal of persuasion to make John go out to a hut near the croft and bring in a 'greybeard' — that is, a big earthenware jar. He was a fine man, this John, a big lanky fellow of sixty with a wonderful fund of old stories. After swearing his guests to secrecy, he had uncorked the greybeard and had poured into tumblers, which had been brought by his niece at Woolworth's in Glasgow, a good stiff three-fingers of the finest whisky that had ever dodged the gaugers and crossed the lips of man. It had warmed the cockles of their hearts so fervently that another peg had gone into the Woolworth tumblers, and John himself had given vent to his elation in song. They had kept it up until midnight, Grant assured me. Until nearly one o'clock Gillespie insisted.

AUGUSTUS MUIR

My eye travelled on a wondrous journey along the glittering jewellery arrayed like a harem of temptresses on the shelves of a Highland hotel bar; seventy-two bottles of golden single malt whisky, each one different, bidding me in silent invitation to taste. After what must have seemed to the barman like several hours, my reeling wheel of fortune stopped at Clynelish, a 12-year-old nectar from Brora in eastern Sutherland.

'Aye,' ventured the barman with characteristic Scots economy, 'they say that one's almost as good as a fine old brandy.'

Almost as good as a fine old brandy! What a gross calumny upon single malt to suggest that at its very apex of maturity, mellowness, roundness and depth, the best to which it can hope to aspire is to stand on the ladder of epicurean achievement one rung below the fiery spirit of the grape. I accused the barman of being ignorant, and possibly even English. 'Well,' he defended huffily, 'I'm a vodka drinker myself.'

ALAN HAMILTON, *THE TIMES*

After a fortnight I received a letter from Neil Quinn, and that letter changed all my plans — changed everything.

'Look where I do be, long man,' he wrote, 'at Uiskavagh, Isle of Skye, on the shores of Loch Eyndale, that runs and winds from the open sea that Stevenson wrote songs about — Skye and Mull and Canna and Eigg and Rum, and Barra low down on the horizon — as famous an archipelago as any in song or story. All about me are the wine-red moors and over every prospect tower the wonderful pinnacles of the mighty Cuchullins Hills. For the sake of the Lord God Almighty come you over and see life with me. And, unlike Kipling, you don't need to buy no 'am neither. There be fish in the waters greedy for mussels: whiting, the chicken of the sea, codling fresh-bearded, haddock marked by Peter's thumb, and torpedo-tailed mackerel; there are lochs in the hills stocked with Loch Leven trout and rainbow-trout and sea-trout that have been transplanted; there are coneys amongst the limestone on the braefaces, and red grouse on the moors, and blue hares a-plenty. Also there is a motor-boat, double-keeled and with a most entertaining engine. And above all there is whisky — Uiskavagh whisky, the finest whisky in the world when drunk in Skye; old as a grown man, mild as your goat's milk, soothing as a woman's hand in your hair, inspiring as a tune — a very great whisky.

MAURICE WALSH, *THE KEY ABOVE THE DOOR*, 1923

In 1972 the Scottish Tourist Board inaugurated the 'Whisky Trail'. The first thing to mention is the guides. At Glenlivet they are clean-cut, kilted young men, mostly students, but at the others they are girls, also students, and as you follow them round in your small group, listening to their careful explanations of the processes, it is impossible for the words 'Highland lassie' not to form in your mind. They are clear-eyed, clear-skinned, frank of demeanour and gentle . . . it does not need the dram at the end of the tour to make one stagger out of the distillery more than half in love. Driving round that beautiful place, past oyster-catchers and curlews, past enormous off-white Charolais bulls like moulded dough, one can become partisan for a particular malt as one can become partisan for a particular football-team, seduced by the splendours of those serious, handsome, intelligent Scottish girl guides.

P. J. KAVANAGH, *SUNDAY TELEGRAPH MAGAZINE*

Lochnagar

The smell of whisky pervaded every corner of the house so powerfully that any teetotaller would have committed a breach of his oath by merely inhaling the air.

JOHN STANHOPE (AGED 19) ON A NINETEENTH CENTURY HIGHLAND INN

We had here (at Fort William) an abundance of excellent goat's milk and whey. Malt liquor is very scarce in Scotland; and what is drank of this kind in the Highlands is, I believe, imported from England. The constant beverage of this country is a nauseous and abominable spirit that is called whisky. The natives are very fond of it.

THE REV. P. HOMER, OBSERVATIONS ON A SHORT TOUR IN THE SUMMER OF 1803 TO THE WESTERN HIGHLANDS OF SCOTLAND

But the breakfasts! that's what redeems the land — and every county has its own peculiar excellence. In Argyllshire, you have the Loch-fine herring, fat, luscious and delicious, just out of the water, falling to pieces with its own richness — melting away like butter in your mouth. In Aberdeenshire, you have the Finnan haddo' with a flavour all its own, vastly relishing — just salt enough to be piquant, without parching you up with thirst. In Perthshire, there is the Tay salmon, kippered, crisp and juicy — a very magnificent morsel — a leetle heavy, but that's easily counteracted by a teaspoonful of the Athole whisky.

SUSAN FERRIER

After dinner, the landlord brought in a genuine Scoth whisky — that nectar of Scotland. It is nothing but very strong corn brandy strongly impregnated however with the characteristic smell of turf which is to be found in all Scotch dwellings and prepared in a peculiar way. A mixture of hot water, sugar and some of this spirit forms an agreeable beverage, which, no doubt, is very pleasant and even beneficial, after a walk or any expedition in the misty moisture of these mountains.

DR CARUS

A man of the Hebrides as soon as he appears in the morning swallows a glass of whisky: yet they are not a drunken race, at least I was never present at much intemperance; but no man is so abstemious as to refuse the morning dram which they call a skalk.

SAMUEL JOHNSON

I have been tempted to think that this spirit has in it, by infusion, the seeds of anger, revenge and murder. This I confess is a little too poetical, but those who drink of it to any degree of excess behave, for the most part, like true barbarians, I think much beyond the effect of other liquors.

EDWARD BURT

Whisky and the Arts

Nearly all the bards have been poor – the children of misfortune. Some have brought discomfort upon themselves by that love of whisky which is so inherent in Scottish minstrels of the lowlier rank.

REV. CHARLES ROGERS

Madam Adelina Patti-Nicolini drinks exclusively at her meals whisky and water; all orators and all persons who require to make use of their voice have adopted in this country this drink. It is therefore not surprising that the House of Commons submit to a severe test such an important part of their daily consumption as whisky. After comparison, it has been decided that Messrs James Buchanan & Co. of Glasgow and London be the sole purveyors of it.

FIGARO, A LONDON NEWSPAPER, APRIL *1888*

The steward placed on the table a syphon and a bottle of whisky which carried the label '*Edouard VIII: Very old Genuine Scotch Whisky: André Bloc et Cie, Saigon*', and the coloured picture of a Regency buck, gazing sceptically at the consumer through a quizzing glass.

    'Alphonse,' said Corker, 'I'm surprised at you.' ·
    'No like?'
    'Bloody well no like.'
    'Whisky-soda,' the man explained patiently, almost tenderly, as though in the nursery. 'Nice.'
    Corker filled his glass, tasted, grimaced.

EVELYN WAUGH, *SCOOP*, 1938

Designing the well-known get-up of "Johnnie Walker" in the "Johnnie Walker" studios

The only 'hard liquor' of any operatic consequence to be mentioned by librettists appears to be whisky. Whisky is the staple diet of everybody in Puccini's *Girl of the Golden West*, where the first act is set in the Polka Bar and orders for drinks all round are frequently made to cries of 'Wisky per tutti!' The hero of the piece, Johnson, makes a considerable impression on everybody on both sides of the footlights by ordering water with his 'wisky'.

Though Puccini composed one opera with a setting in the British Isles, he kept his whisky exclusively for his American characters. Thus in the first act of *Madam Butterfly* we find Lieutenant Pinkerton offering the American Consul a choice of 'milk-punch or wisky'. Sharpless, being no fool, chose 'wisky', thus proving without question that the Scotch whisky trade was a flourishing dollar-earner more than fifty years

ago. At least I presume it was Scotch and not one of those remarkable Japanese brands 'as supplied to HRH King Victoria'.

SPIKE HUGHES IN THE *COMPLEAT IMBIBER*

Went from Glasgow to Paisley, and to No. 5 Maxwellton Street to Lachlan MacNeill, shoemaker; found him and Hector installed in a small public, both rather screwed, Hector the worse. They have been at the tale of O'Kane's leg for about a week and Hector has made about 62 sheets of Gaelic x 4 = 248, say about 260 pages of foolscap.

DIARY ENTRY FOR AUGUST 17 1870 BY JOHN FRANCIS CAMPBELL OF ISLAY, THE COLLECTOR OF GAELIC FOLKLORE

Macdonald, one of our actors in Bass's troupe, Dundee, always carried a large-sized bamboo cane, at all times his companion. We were crossing the river Tay ferry in a boat from Dundee, careworn, hungry and tired; no money, salaries unpaid; yet Jemmy Macdonald seemed little to feel it. There came no repinings from him; this was a riddle to us starvelings. Aboard the boat he whispered to me: 'Laddie come abaft' *sotto voce*. 'Not a word, laddie', unscrewing his bamboo, the top a cup, the stick a whisky bottle. 'Tak a drink, laddie — real Glenlivet; nae excise-man ever took gauge of this whisky.' In the stick lay 'Jemmy's' hilarity. Doubtless many of us find comfort in the stick at times.

EDWARD STIRLING *OLD DRURY LANE*, 1881

'My future,' said the Master, 'is a subject—to me—of inexhaustible interest. I would willingly hear you dilate on it for hours. But I have to be at the theatre before six. We must have tea.'

I had not expected a cuppa. That would have been *mal à propos*. Crumbling an image. I hadn't bargained though for what I was hospitably offered.

A bottle of Scotch. Dry gingers. Baby sodas. Ice. And a Lalique bowl full of succulent French nougat.

EDGAR LUSTGARTEN TAKING TEA WITH NOEL COWARD IN 1929, IN *THE COMPLEAT IMBIBER*

It takes a Celtic mind to appreciate that the last drink is not the final one. The late Sir Harry Lauder had several farewell world tours before he retired. Newspapermen in Fleet Street who invented the Final, Late Final, Latest, Extra, and Late Extra were undoubtedly of Caledonian extraction. To have an edition after the Final may seem ridiculous to the stolid Teuton or the logical Gaul, but to the Highlander such things are a matter of hoots-moreover, and so it is with drinks.

Everybody knows the phrase for the last drink of whisky, which Sir Harry Lauder popularized in song. 'Just a Wee Deoch an Doruis'. The phrase is pronounced 'Joch and Dorish', and means, 'A Drink at the Door'. The real point is that 'A Drink at the Door' is quite non-committal. It does not state on oath that it is positively the last drink. It leaves room for equivocation, and equivocation is the life-blood of the Gael, apart from whisky.

PHILIP MACKIE, IN *THE COMPLEAT IMBIBER*

In 1933 Dame Ethel Smythe, then aged 75, visited Barra and spent two days with Sir Compton Mackenzie. She was very deaf, but as active as one of the Barra ponies that ran wild on the machair:

Father John Macmillan arranged for a waulking at the little parish hall of Northbay. This is the vigorous ceremony of shrinking the tweed. On either side of a trestle table sat six women who swayed backwards and forwards as they lifted a length of tweed and banged it down on the table and rolled it towards one another; the length of tweed would have been previously dipped in urine. Usually one of the women sings a waulking song of verse after verse while this is being done.

When the exhausting process was over Dame Ethel asked Father John if it would be in order for her to offer the women a dram.

He replied, 'Yes, indeed, but I'm afraid there isn't a dram to offer them.'

'Oh yes, there is,' said Dame Ethel, as she lifted her skirt and produced from a pocket on the inside of it a bottle of whisky with which she went round filling the dram-glasses fetched from the hall pantry.

'How do you say good health in Gaelic?' she asked me.

'Slainte mhàth,' I shouted.

'Can't hear you.'

Simultaneously Father John and I bellowed 'Slainte mhàth.'

'Can't hear you. Never mind. Good health to all you nice people and thank you for giving me such a splendid evening.'

She left for Lochboisdale next evening and sent a bottle of whisky to Father John from Castlebay.

'A noble glorious woman,' he declared in his richest tones, with which the pop of the cork seemed to express enthusiastic agreement.

COMPTON MACKENZIE

Desmond MacCarthy had got me a fine full-time job on the BBC . . . I had four years with an immense salary and the chance to find work for Dylan (Thomas).

Dylan had only one weakness – he could not read correct poets like Pope or Dryden. He was at his best at the 'wild and woolly' poets. I used to keep him on beer all day till he had done his night's work and then take him down to the duty room where the charming Miss Backhouse or Miss Tofield would pour us both a treble whisky for our labours. It was with Blake and Manley Hopkins that Dylan became almost Superman; but we had bad luck with Dryden. Dylan had got at the whisky first and he started behaving like a prima donna. He insisted on having an announcer instead of beginning the programme right away as we used to on the Third Programme. There were only two minutes to go and I rushed back to the studio and found Dylan snoring in front of the mike with only twenty seconds left. He was slumped back in his chair, with an almost seraphic expression of blissful peace. I shook him awake, and, to his horror and consternation, began announcing him, not in my South African accent, but trying to talk like an English announcer, with my tonsils, in an 'Oxford accent'. Dylan nearly jumped out of his skin with fright and horror, and was almost sober when he got the green light, though he did bungle the title as 'Ode on Shaint Sheshilia's Day'; but after that his voice cleared up and I began to breathe again.

RAYNER HEPPENSTALL

We went to the Cottage and took some Whiskey — I wrote a sonnet for the mere sake of writing some lines under the Roff — they are so bad I cannot transcribe them — The Man at the Cottage was a great Bore with his Anecdotes — I hate the Rascal — his Life consists in fuz, fuzzy, fuzziest — He drinks glasses five for the quarter and twelve for the hour, — he is a mahogany faced old Jackass who knew Burns — He ought to have been kicked for having spoken to him. He calls himself 'a curious old Bitch' — but he is a flat old Dog — should like to employ Caliph Vatheck to kick him — O the flummery of a birth place! Cant! Cant! Cant! It is enough to give a spirit the guts-ache — Many a true word they say is spoken in jest — this may be because his Gab hindered my sublimity. — The flat dog made me write a flat sonnet.

KEATS, LETTER TO JOHN HAMILTON REYNOLDS, JULY 1818

Then we proceeded to the Cottage he was born in — there was a board to that effect by the door side — it had the same effect as the same sort of memorial at Stratford on Avon — We drank some Toddy to Burns's Memory with an old Man who knew Burns — damn him and damn his Anecdotes — he was a great bore — it was impossible for a Southern to understand above 5 words in a hundred — There was something good in his description of Burns's melancholy the last time he saw him. I was determined to write a sonnet in the Cottage — I did — but it is so bad I cannot venture it here.

KEATS, LETTER TO HIS BROTHER TOM, 10 JULY 1818

Burns' Cottage

Whisky and Royalty

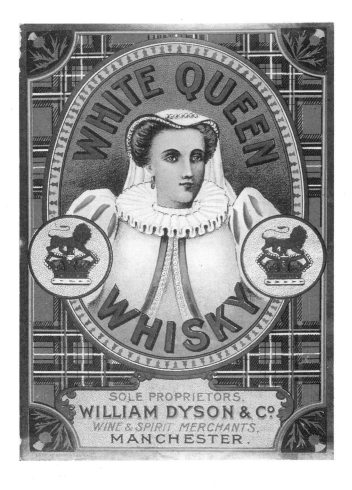

This autumn [1822] King George the Fourth visited Scotland. The whole country went mad. The Clan Grant had quite a triumph, no equipage was as handsome as that of Colonel Francis Grant, our acting chief, in their red and green and gold. There were processions, a review, a levée, a drawing-room, and a ball. Lord Conyngham, the Chamberlain, was looking everywhere for pure Glenlivet whisky; the King drank nothing else. It was not to be had out of the Highlands. My father sent word to me — I was the cellarer — to empty my pet bin, where was whisky long in wood, long in uncorked bottles, mild as milk, and the true contraband *goût* in it. Much as I grudged this treasure it made our fortunes afterwards, showing on what trifles great events depend. The whisky, and fifty brace of ptarmigan all shot by one man, went up to Holyrood House, and were graciously received and made much of, and a reminder of this attention at a proper moment by the gentlemanly Chamberlain ensured to my father the Indian Judgeship.

ELIZABETH GRANT OF ROTHIEMURCHUS

On receiving the poet on the quarter deck, His Majesty called for a bottle of Highland whisky, and having drunk his health in this national liquor, desired a glass to be filled for him. Sir Walter, after draining his own bumper, made a request that the King would condescend to bestow on him the glass out of which his Majesty had just drunk his health; and this being granted, the precious vessel was immediately wrapped up and carefully deposited in what he conceived to be the safest part of his dress. So he returned with it to Castle Street but on reaching his house he found a guest established there of a sort rather different from the usual visitors of the time — the poet Crabbe. Scott entering, wet and hurried, embraced the venerable man with brotherly affection. The royal gift was forgotten — he sat down beside Crabbe, and the glass was crushed to atoms. His scream and gesture made his wife conclude that he had sat down on a pair of scissors: but very little harm had been done except the breaking of the glass of which he alone had been thinking.

J. G. LOCKHART

I wrote a note on the 11th September to Mr G. E. Anson (Her Majesty's Private Secretary) stating that the distillery was now in full operation, and would be so until six o'clock next day, and knowing how anxious HRH Prince Albert was to patronize and make himself acquainted with everything of a mechanical nature, I said I should feel much pleasure in showing him the works. The note was handed in at Balmoral Castle about 9pm. Next day about four o'clock, whilst in the house, I observed Her Majesty and the Prince Consort approaching. I ran and opened the door, when the Prince said, 'We have come to see through your works Mr Begg.' There were besides, HRH the Prince of Wales, the Princess Royal, and Prince Alfred, accompanied by Lady Cumming. I at once conducted the Royal Party to the distillery.

On entering the works, the two young Princes at once ran away among the casks, like any other children, whereupon Her Majesty called them, 'Where are you young children going?' on which I laid hold of one in each hand, and held them during the time they remained.

I endeavoured to explain the whole process of malting, brewing and distilling, showing the Royal Party the bere in its original state, and in all its different stages of manufacture until it came out at the mouth of the still pipe in spirits. HRH tasted the spirits with his finger from both the still pipes. On going downstairs HRH turned round to me and said (looking at the locks on the stills), 'I see you have got your locks there.' On my replying, 'These are the Queen's locks', Her Majesty took a hearty laugh.

When we came to the door I asked HRH if he would like to taste the spirit in its matured state, as we had cleared some that day from bond, which I thought was very fine. HRH having agreed to this, I called for a bottle and glasses (which had been previously in readiness) and, presenting one glass to Her Majesty, she tasted it. So also did his Royal Highness the Prince. I then presented a glass to the Princess Royal, and to the Prince of Wales, and Prince Alfred, all of whom tasted the spirit.

HRH the Prince of Wales was going to carry his glass quickly to his mouth. I checked him, saying it was very strong, so he did not take but a very small drop of it. Afterwards the Royal Party took their departure, I thanking them for the honour of the visit they had been so generous to pay the distillery.

DIARY OF JOHN BEGG, PROPRIETOR OF LOCHNAGAR, 1848

Brown had a primary appetite – for whisky. When he was young and living an active, out-of-door life his drinking made little difference. Brought indoors, and given next to nothing to do, whisky began to affect him. The Queen liked whisky herself and drank it neat, or in her tea, or with Apollinaris water. Doubtless her mind was on something else at the time but the astonished Gladstone once saw her lace a very respectable claret with some of Begg's best. She did not drink much herself, but long custom had rather made her come to expect it of her beloved highlanders, and she was especially indulgent to her friend Brown.

Two stories about his drinking went round the Court. At Balmoral he failed to appear one day to sit on the box of her carriage. The Private Secretary went at once to Brown's room and found him totally incapable of climbing on to anything, let alone a carriage-box. With great kindness he himself took Brown's place, and the Queen merely ordered the coachman to proceed and made no other comment. On another occasion at Balmoral, Brown was tipsy and he stumbled and fell flat. The Queen instantly announced that she, too, had felt an earth tremor.

TYLER WHITTLE

At the glittering champagne reception thrown by the British Ambassador to Hungary during the interval of the Royal Ballet's performance of *Manon* at the Budapest State Opera House Princess Margaret was in danger of having a dry run.

A royal aide pointed out to the 'dips' that she favours whisky and water rather than a glass of bubbly. A discreet gentleman from the Foreign Office thereupon gallantly smuggled a bottle under his dinner jacket into the building to rescue the parched Princess.

DAILY TELEGRAPH, APRIL 1985

After Queen Victoria visited Long John Macdonald at his Ben Nevis distillery in 1848 the following piece of intelligence appeared in the April issue of the *Illustrated London News*:

Mr Macdonald has presented a cask of whisky to Her Majesty and an order has been sent to the Treasury to permit the spirits to be removed to the cellars of Buckingham Palace free of duty. The cask is not to be opened until His Royal Highness the Prince of Wales attains his majority [in 1863].

Balmoral Castle

Royal Lochnagar Distillery

In Queen Victoria's reign whenever anyone went out stalking, a whole bottle of whisky was given out, and whatever the guest did not drink became the perquisite of the stalker. It was quite a common thing for a stalker to come to the Castle and drink off a glass of neat whisky before he started. Of course if he went out stalking no harm was done, but when the weather was impossible and the mist came down he retired to his house and started the day slightly intoxicated. The amount of whisky consumed by the servants was truly stupendous. Whenever the Queen went out driving, a bottle of whisky was put under the coachman's seat and was supposed to provide stimulant to anyone who had an accident. It was said that early in the Queen's reign a poor man had been found at the side of the road in a state of exhaustion and that Her Majesty had remarked what a pity it was that no one had any stimulant to revive him. This was at once rectified and innumerable bottles of whisky must have gone astray in this way. But the whole atmosphere was wrong. A drunken man was so common that no one ever remarked on it.

Another occasion when whisky was given freely was the anniversary of the Prince Consort's birthday. All the stalkers, gillies, and people on the estate were expected to attend dressed in top-hats (what the people called a funeral hat) and black coats. A prayer was said in front of the Prince Consort's statue, and the Queen drove there in her carriage with two grey horses and an outrider. Then whisky was sent out as light refreshment at the back of the wood. The result was that the whole community was three parts intoxicated and when we went for a walk in the afternoon it was no uncommon sight to find a man in a top-hat and frock-coat fast asleep in the woods.

SIR FREDERICK PONSONBY

Whisky and Religion

The site wheron the Distillery now stands was the place where the famous Magnus Eunson carried on his operations. This man was the greatest and most accomplished smuggler in Orkney. By profession he was a U.P. Church Officer, and kept a stock of illicit whisky under the pulpit, but in reality he was a '*non Professing*' distiller. This godly person was accustomed to give out the psalms in a more unctuous manner than usual if the excise officers were in church, as he knew that he was suspected, and that a party of the revenue officers, taking advantage of his absence, might at that moment be searching his house.

A singular story is told of this man. Hearing that the church was to be searched for whisky by a new party of excisemen, Eunson had all the kegs removed to his house, placed in the middle of an empty room, and covered with a white clean cloth. As the officers approached after their unsuccessful search in the church, Eunson gathered all his people, including the maidservants, round the whisky, which, with its covering of white, under which a coffin lid had been placed, looked like a bier.

Eunson knelt at the head with the Bible in his hand and the others with their psalm books. As the door opened they set up a wail for the dead, and Eunson made a sign to the officers that it was a death, and one of the attendants whispered 'smallpox'. Immediately the officer and his men made off as fast as they could and left the smuggler for some time in peace.

ALFRED BARNARD, VISITING HIGHLAND PARK

Mr John Maitland, chyrurgeon for the Soule . . . a Presbyter of the Episcopal church of Scotland was attached to Lord Ogilvie's regiment in the service of Prince Charles, 1745. He administered the Holy Eucharist to Lord Strathallan on the Culloden field, it is said, with oat-cake and whisky, the requisite elements not being attainable.

BISHOP FORBES

A clergyman was administering consolation to a dying Highlander when he was shocked by the patient asking him if there 'was any whisky in heaven?' Half apologetically he added 'Ye ken, sir, it's not that I care for it, but it looks weel on the table.'

ALEXANDER HISLOP

I remember the first funeral I saw fifty years ago in the Highlands. It was in the old graveyard of Kilchrist, Skye, where a large company of crofters had gathered from all parts of the parish of Strath. There was a confused undertone of conversation audible at a little distance as I passed along the public road; and as soon as I came in sight two or three of the mourners at once made for me, carrying bottle, glasses, and a plate of bits of cake. Though I was an entire stranger to them and to the deceased, I knew enough of Highland customs and feelings to be assured that on no account could I be excused from at least tasting the refreshments. The halt of a few minutes showed me that much whisky was being consumed around the ruined kirk.

SIR ARCHIBALD GEIKIE, *SCOTTISH REMINISCENCES*

Bernard always had a few prayers in the hall and some whiskey afterwards as he was rarther pious but Mr Salteena was not very addicted to prayers so he marched up to bed.

DAISY ASHFORD

We're a' dry wi' the drinkin' o't,
We're a' dry wi' the drinkin' o't,
The minister kisst the fiddler's wife,
He couldna preach for thinkin' o't.

TRIBUTE TO WHISKY

'This is no' a godly place at all, at all,' said a discontented labourer in the Perthshire Highlands. 'They dinna preach the gospel here — and they wahtter the whusky!'

SIR ARCHIBALD GEIKIE

Yesterday we were invited to the funeral of an old lady, and found ourselves in the midst of fifty people, who were regaled with a sumptuous feast, accompanied by the music of a dozen pipers. In short, this meeting had all the air of a grand festival; and the guests did such honour to the entertainment that many of them could not stand when we were reminded of the business on which we had met . . .

By midnight there was not a sober person in the family, the females excepted . . . Our entertainer was a little chagrined at our retreat, and seemed to think it a disparagement to his family, that not above a hundred gallons of whisky had been drunk upon such a solemn occasion.

TOBIAS SMOLLETT

Whisky, no doubt, is a devil; but why has this devil so many worshippers?

LORD COCKBURN

The funeral expenses of Hugh Campbell of Calder, in 1616, amounted to £1,647 16s 4d. This expenditure included a charge for whisky equal to one-fourth of the amount.

REV. CHARLES ROGERS

At funerals four rounds of whisky were considered due to wounded affection and departed worth, and respect was shown to the dead by the intoxication of the living.

REV. ROBERT STORY

There is a story about two rival distillery owners named Grant who encountered each other at a mutual Grant relation's funeral on a bitterly cold day. They were waiting for the funeral procession to arrive at the graveside when one offered the other his flask and remarked:

'Ye may as well have a dram, ye'll not often get the opportunity of anything as good.'

The other took a good swallow and returned the flask poker-faced with the reply:

'Man, that's just what I required. I'd have brought my own flask, but I don't want it said I smelled of whisky at the funeral.'

MICHAEL BRANDER

Going to a Funeral   Returning from a Funeral

Whisky as Medicine

JAMES BUCHANAN & Cº
SCOTCH WHISKY DISTILLERS.

But long did we think e'er our sportsmen came
    hame,
To rest and partake of our highland game,
We lost expectation to see them that night,
And thought they were gone to Marr Lodge till
    daylight,
But at ten of evening, being a dreadful rain,
Who rapped at our door but our gallant sportsmen,
So faintish with hunger, with cold and with rain,
So tir'd and benumb'd they could scarcely win ben,
We flew to our whisky, which proved a cure ever,
And gave each a jugful that warmed their liver,
Some hours at the ingle did dry their outside,
After cock-brue and toddy, all went to bed.

JAMES CHRISTIE, GAMEKEEPER, *INSTRUCTIONS FOR HUNTING*, 1817

Ah, a man feels young in Glendochart even at the age of ninety. If you will but live your life out of doors in this envied valley, fishing-rod in hand in summer, and gun or curling-stone in winter, you can put behind you all fear of ill-health or old age and even, if so inclined, like the sturdy and ancient Don Malloch, drink whisky with impunity every day and all day long.

E. E. BRIGGS

In Scotland which abounds with lakes and inlets of the sea, and high mountains that occasion frequent rains, the moderate use of Spirituous Liquors has been reckoned cherishing, and in some degree necessary; and, accordingly, the most of the people in it have been long in the habit of drinking them in moderate degree, and many of these live to great ages in very good health.

SEAFIELD MSS, 1751

'By Cot, it is the only liquor fit for a gentleman to drink in the morning, if he can have the good fortune to come by it, you see.'

'Or after dinner either, Captain,' added the Doctor. 'It is worth all the wines of France for flavour and more cordial to the system besides.'

SIR WALTER SCOTT. SIR BINGO ENTERTAINS THE CAPTAIN AND THE DOCTOR

Gie me the real Glenlivet, and I weel believe I could mak' drinking toddy oot o' sea-water. The human mind never tires o' Glenlivet, any mair than o' caller air. If a body could just find oot the exac' proportion and quantity that ought to be drunk every day and keep to that, I verily trow that he might leeve for ever, without dying at a', and that doctors and kirkyards would go oot o' fashion.

JOHN WILSON, PROFESSOR OF MORAL PHILOSOPHY WRITING UNDER THE PEN NAME OF 'CHRISTOPHER NORTH', *NOCTES AMBROSIANAE*, 1827. DIALOGUE ATTRIBUTED TO JAMES HOGG, THE ETTRICK SHEPHERD

The old and the new. *Top*, one of Bell's first labels, issued in 1904, and *bottom* their current label

I have drunk (whisky) for nearly seventy years without detriment to my constitution. A couple of years ago, I underwent a major operation and when the doctor came to change my dressings for the last time he sounded me thoroughly and said all my organs were in a condition that would do credit to a man quarter my age and there was no reason why I shouldn't live to be a hundred!

HUGH MACDIARMID

In the First World War I served in Salonika for a couple of years. There was little real fighting; the main enemy was disease and the consequent casualties were immensely greater than any incurred on the battlefields.

The principal causes were dysentery, blackwater fever and malaria. It was noted that when there was whisky in the officers' or sergeants' messes there were few recurrences of malaria but when whisky was not available the recurrence-rate shot up at once.

HUGH MACDIARMID

"WHISKY HAS KILLED MORE MEN THAN BULLETS."
"MAYBE — BUT I'D RATHER BE FULL O' WHISKY THAN FULL O' BULLETS!"

When America went dry on 16 January 1920 the only way to procure whisky legally was by waving a doctor's prescription; the more medicinal-tasting whiskies were in great demand. White Horse Distillers ran a series of advertisements featuring medical men drinking Scotch with their patients. A typical caption featuring a cut glass decanter and tumbler beside a sculpture of a white horse read:

The Doctor came round last night! Settled the affairs of the nation. Then said he must be getting along. And then a word was whispered to the Doctor which he might never have heard before. 'Well perhaps now that you mention it,' said the Doctor.

'You know, Doctor, I do think whatever else a man's particular about he ought to be particular about his whisky. Now I'm a White Horse man. So's my old father. Says it's a good heart tonic. And I've heard you say the same thing yourself about White Horse. If you ask me, it's a first-class digestive too. It's so mellow! Not a touch of fire in it — and yet what a glow.'

As Keats might have said, 'clever stuff'.

When the Eighteenth Amendment was repealed the Distillers Company took large advertisements in the British press to reassure their home consumers that supplies were ample and they reminded the world that:

There is no purer drink than Scotch Whisky. It is the purified essence of malted barley, and was called by the early distillers Usquebaugh, which means the Water of Life. It is enjoyable; it is healthful; it places no strain on the digestion; it is an excellent tonic. It is recognized as one of the major amenities of civilization.

Beying moderately taken
it cutteth fleume,
it lighteneth the mynd,
it quickeneth the spirits,
it cureth the hydropsie,
it pounceth the stone,
it repelleth the gravel,
it puffeth away ventositie,
it kepyth and preserveth
the eyes from dazelying,
the tongue from lispying,
the teethe from chatterying,
the throte from rattlying,
the weasan from stieflying,
the stomach from womblying,
the harte from swellying,
the bellie from wirtching,
the guts from rumblying,
the hands from shivering,
the sinews from shrinkying,
the veynes from crumplying,
the bones from akying,
the marrow from soakying,
and truly it is a sovereign liquor
if it be ordlie taken.

RAPHAEL HOLINSHED, 1564

When the wisdom of Parliament was first addressed to the great question: 'What is Whisky?' it appointed a committee presided over by Doctor Playfair before whom a very knowledgeable scientist gave evidence. To him Doctor Playfair addressed the question, 'Had not science established that it is impossible by any chemical test to draw a distinction between Whisky made naturally (which at the time of the inquiry meant a pot still) and that made artificially?' The witness agreed.

'Then how do you dare to suggest that there is a difference between the two products?'

'I have an infallible test of my own,' replied the witness.

'And what might that be?' asked the scornful Doctor Playfair.

'The state of my head the next morning,' replied the witness.

MAURICE HEALY

Nor does the home-spun juice of malt,
Like foreign wines, alone exalt
The fancy, but if drank in season
Strengthens and modulates our reason.

For men of sense must own 'tis better
To drink good Malt, than starve on water.

ANON

An old friend of mine who used to go with the Hoylake men for matches with the Lothian clubs told me that there was a dinner every night of the visit, at which a bottle of whisky was set before each man and finished during the evening. But all were early and steady on the tee next morning.

IVOR BROWN

The event of New Year's Day itself was the game of shinty. One game I remember* was captained on the one side by a man of sixty years of age and the other by a sixty-two year old. They had been opposing captains for years and the closest of friends all their lives. Both were over six feet and as lean as a lath. They met on the field of play about eleven o'clock, each carrying his trusty home-made *caman*. Of course several drams had already been down and many *slainte mhaths* and *bliadhna-mhaths ùrs* (good healths and good New Years) had been exchanged.

Skin and hair went flying in real style. A bloody face or limb was a mark of honour and by the end of two hours' fierce encounter few indeed were scathless. Generous 'revivers' were resorted to frequently during the match, but so hard was the game that every man was as sober as a judge by one o'clock, and partook of an amazing meal of broth and beef and potatoes which the goodwife of the house had prepared in three large washing-pots.

COLIN MACDONALD
    * period is late nineteenth century

All that is contended for in behalf of the Highlanders is that he shall have liberty on moderate terms suited to the poverty of his circumstances to convert the growth of his own soil through his personal industry to the necessary beverage of wholesome spirit, whether diluted with water as grog or taken as a cordial dram to brace sometime the humid — sometimes the bleak piercing winds of the North.

JOHN GRANT OF BALNAGOWN, 1798

Little variation seems to have taken place in the manner of living since the time of Dr Johnson. In the Hebrides they still continue to take their *streah*, or glass of whisky, before breakfast, which, though by no means a palatable regimen to Englishmen, seems at least to be a very wholesome one, if one may judge from the healthy appearance and ruddy skins of the natives — indeed, in such a wet climate, it is almost absolutely necessary to drink spirits in some degree. Additional *streahs* are never refused in the daytime.

JOHN STANHOPE

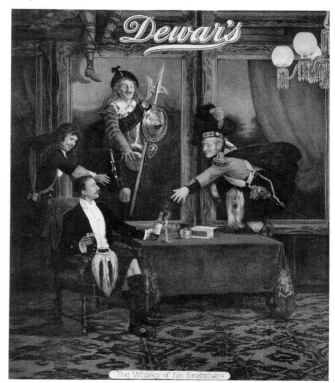
The Whisky of his forefathers

Dewar was the first whisky man to set out single-handed to conquer the world. In a two-year journey he visited twenty-six countries and acquired thirty-two agencies: I was going through a 'prohibition' State (in Canada) and tried to get some whisky from the conductor of the train, but without success. However he eventually advised me to try at a store at the next stopping place and this I did.

'Do you sell whisky?'

'Are you sick, mister, or got a medical certificate?'

'No.'

'Then I can't do it; but I reckon our cholera mixture'll about fix you. Try a bottle of that.'

I did but to my great astonishment received a very familiar bottle which, although it was labelled on one side 'Cholera Mixture: a wineglassful to be taken every two hours, or oftener as required' had upon the other side the well-known label of a firm of Scotch whisky distillers whose name modesty requires me to suppress.

THOMAS DEWAR

I have made a careful and exhaustive analysis of Messrs W&S Strong's Real Mountain Dew Finest Scotch Whisky, and find the same to be an Old and Well-Matured Spirit, free from impurity, and possessing a fine aroma and taste. It is a clear and well-blended whisky of the best class.

TESTIMONIAL FROM DR IVISON MACADAM OF THE SURGEON'S HALL, EDINBURGH WHICH USED TO APPEAR ON THE LABEL OF REAL MOUNTAIN DEW IN MORE LIBERAL TIMES

It is prescribed by the medical faculty as, on the whole, safer drink than much of the wine that comes from abroad. If one were asked to name the two most conspicuous gifts which Scotland has made in recent times to the United Kingdom, one could hardly go wrong in answering Whisky and Golf.

SIR ARCHIBALD GEIKIE

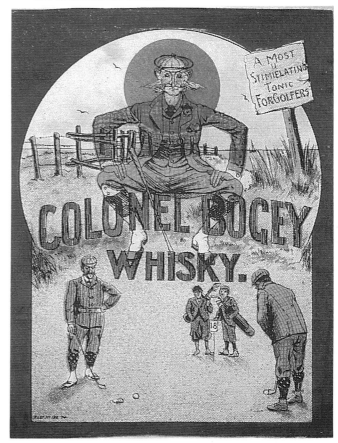

The Highlanders . . . regale themselves with whisky; a malt spirit as strong as geneva, which they swallow in great quantities without any signs of inebriation. They are used to it from the cradle and find it an excellent preservative against the winter cold which must be extreme on these mountains. I am told that it is given with great success to infants as a cordial in the confluent smallpox when the eruption seems to flag and the symptoms grow unfavourable.

TOBIAS SMOLLETT

The northern nations are more addicted to the use of strong liquors than the southern, in order to supply by art the want of that genial warmth of blood which the sun produces.

JAMES BOSWELL

Alake, quo Neil, I'm frail an' auld,
And find my bluid gros unco cauld,
I think it makes me blythe and bauld,
A wee drop Highland whisky, O.
But a' the doctors do agree
That whisky's no the drink for me,
I'm fleyed they'll gar me tyne my glee,
Should they part me and whisky, O.

AGNES LYONS, WIFE OF DR LYONS, MINISTER OF GLAMIS: NEIL GOW'S FAREWELL TO WHISKY

I was born below par to th'extent of two whiskies.

C. E. MONTAGUE

In view of the statements frequently made as to present medical opinion regarding alcohol and alcoholic beverages we the undersigned think it desirable to issue the following statement, a statement which we believe represents the teaching of leading clinical teachers as well as that of the great majority of medical practitioners.

Recognizing that in prescribing alcohol the requirement of the individual must be the governing rule, we are convinced of the correctness of the opinion so long and generally held that alcohol is a rapid and trustworthy restorative. In many cases it can be truly said to be truly life saving owing to its power to sustain cardiac and nervous energy while protecting the wasting nitrogenous tissues. As an article of diet we hold the universal belief of civilized mankind that the moderate use of alcoholic beverages is for adults usually beneficial, amply justified.

We deplore the evils arising from the use of alcoholic beverages. But it is obvious that there is nothing however beneficial which does not in excess become injurious.

STATEMENT SIGNED BY SIXTEEN OF BRITAIN'S LEADING MEDICAL MEN IN *THE LANCET*, 1907

Mary Macleod, the Skye poetess, died in 1705 at the age of 105 giving praise to the thrice-distilled island whisky:
Ho ro, how I enjoy the dram!
Many a person is indebted to it.

Toddies

Duncan Dhu made haste to bring out the pair of pipes that was his principal possession, and to set before his guests the mutton-ham and a bottle of that drink which they call Athole Brose and which is made of old whisky, strained honey and sweet cream, slowly beaten together in the right order and proportion.

R. L. STEVENSON

The laird of Milnain, near Alness, visited his neighbour the laird of Nonikiln. Time wore on, and the visit was prolonged until late at night. At last the sugar got done, and toddy is not very palatable without sugar. In those days no shop was nearer than Tain or Dingwall, and it was too late to send anywhere for a supply. Convivialities were threatened with an abrupt termination when a happy thought found its way into Nonikiln's befogged brain. He had bee-hives in the garden, and honey was an excellent substitute for sugar. A skep was fetched in, the bees were robbed, and the toddy bowl was replenished. The operation was repeated until the bees, revived by the warmth of the room, showed signs of activity, and stung their spoilers into sobriety.

IAN MACDONALD

Take your toddy to bed, put a bowler hat at the foot and drink until you see two.

OLD CURE FOR THE COMMON COLD

Atholl brose is a concoction which is drunk in company and on festive occasions like Hogmanay and St Andrew's Day. There are various receipts, but the simplest method is to mix an equal quantity of running heather honey and fine oatmeal in a little cold water. Then, according to the number of your guests, pour in very slowly a well-flavoured malt whisky. Stir the whole contents vigorously until a generous froth rises to the top. Then bottle and cork tightly, keep for two days and serve in the finest silver bowl that you possess. A pound of oatmeal and a pound of honey will need four pints of whisky.

SIR ROBERT BRUCE LOCKHART

Put a pound of dripped honey into a basin and add sufficient cold water to dissolve it. Stir with a *silver* spoon, and when the water and the honey are well mixed, add gradually one and a half pints of whisky, alias mountain dew. Stir briskly till a froth begins to rise. Bottle and keep tightly corked. Sometimes the yolk of an egg is beat up in the brose.

MEG DOD'S RECIPE FOR ATHOLE BROSE, 1826

First you put in whisky to make it strong; then you add water to make it weak; next you put in lemon to make it sour, then you put in sugar to make it sweet. You put in more whisky to kill the water. Then you say 'here's to you' — and you drink it yourself.

RECIPE FOR TODDY DEVISED BY M. BALEIEV. FOUNDER OF THE MOSCOW CHAUVE-SOURIS COMPANY AS RELATED TO SIR ROBERT BRUCE LOCKHART

Four be the elements;
Here we assemble 'em
Each of man's world
Or existence an emblem.

Press from the lemon
The slow flowing juices —
Bitter is Life
In its lessons and uses!

Bruise the fair sugar lumps —
Nature intended
Her sweet and severe
To be everywhere blended.

Pour the still water —
Unwarning by sound,
Eternity's ocean
Is dark'ning around!

Mingle the Spirit
The life of the bowl! —
Man is cold mortar
Unwarmed by a soul.

Drink of the stream
Ere its potency goes —
No bath is refreshing
Except while it glows.

RHYMING RECIPE FOR TODDY

In fancy I drink once again
— Not drinking whisky and soda
As an Englishman does, which is very ull,
But with all the splendid old ritual,
The urn, the rummers, the smaller glasses,
The silver ladles, and the main essentials.
The whisky toddy is mixed in a rummer,
A round-bottomed tumbler on a stem,
And transferred at intervals with a silver ladle
Into an accompanying wine-glass
By way of cooling it
Sufficiently for consumption
— *Ah! quam dulce est meminisse!*
— We have fallen upon lean days.
Would Burns have sparkled upon small ale
And how would the Ettrick Shepherd
Who took his whisky in a jug
Fare in a time like this?

HUGH MACDIARMID

As for making of toddy, each man must make it to his own taste. To the whisky, the only additions are hot water and sugar: and there are those who declare it is the whisky that must be added to the other two, with more of the whisky and hot water being added turn about until the tumbler is full. That the tumbler itself must be heated to start with, goes without saying.

AUGUSTUS MUIR

Willie an' I cam' doun by Blair
And in by Tullibardine,
The Rye were at the waterside;
An' bee-skeps in the garden;
I saw the reek of a private still—
Says I, 'Gud Lord, I thank ye!'
As Willie and I cam' in by Blair
And out by Killiecrankie.

Ye hinny bees, ye smuggler lads,
Thou, Muse, the bard's protector,
I never kent what Rye was for
Till I had drunk the nectar!
And shall I never drink it mair?
Gud troth, I beg your pardon!
The neist time I come doun by Blair
And in by Tullibardine.

R. L. STEVENSON, ATHOLE BROSE

Deoch-an-Doruis

The whisky trail I still remember is much shorter than the one signposted with such care by the AA through the Speyside area of Scotland. AA stands for Automobile Association, not Alcoholics Anonymous, and the familiar black-and-yellow signs had beckoned me through the gates of Glen Grant in the little village of Rothes.

Rothes is not far from the sea and lies near the famous barley-growing plains of Moray. 'And that,' said Dougie McKessek, the managing director, 'is why the area was selected by Major James Grant in 1840 as the site of what is now one of the most famous single malts in the world.

'And now I wonder if you would like a wee walk?' Firmly he steered me round the back of the distillery, through the orchard and along the banks of the ice-cold burn, whose waters help to make Glen Grant whisky what it is.

The trail led into a small valley, planted in Victorian times with fruit trees and rhododendrons. Finally, there was room only for the burn, which tumbled and chattered between a cleft in the smooth, brown rocks that were slippery with lichen. McKessek gave a conspiratorial wink. 'Would you like a wee dram?'

I looked round the empty landscape. It could hardly have looked more dramless if it tried. But McKessek produced a massive bunch of keys from his pocket, clambered down the bank and opened a safe cunningly let into a rock above the rushing waters and totally concealed by shrubbery. Out came two glasses, a bottle of 20 year-old malt which had been drawn straight from the wood as a special bottling and a small tube, sealed at one end and with a long piece of string attached to the other.

With this primitive device, he brought up a measure of beautifully cold water from the burn to add to the whisky in our glasses. It went down a treat. Subdued Scottish colours turned suddenly hectic. The world turned over and came the right way up again. And that, I told myself, was what they meant when they talked about the whisky trail.

WILLIAM FOSTER, 'IN BRITAIN', APRIL 1980

Glenmorangie is very different: it has a special kind of floweriness, a delicate yet unmistakable fragrance, that I find extremely attractive. It is equally good as a pre-prandial and as a post-prandial drink and I confess that I have drunk it at many other times as well. There is a Glenmorangie which I have drunk at the distillery which is older and more full-bodied than that which is available bottled, possessing more richness and less delicacy than the latter. It goes for blending, of course, but anyone lucky enough to get a dram of it at the distillery will have a memorable experience.

DAVID DAICHES

The world asks for whisky — and soda, and the syphon destroys the work of the still. No more effectual way of ruining the flavour of a good whisky could have been imagined than this one of drowning it in a fizzing solution of carbonic acid gas.

AENEAS MACDONALD

Thee, Ferintosh! O sadly lost!
Scotland lament frae coast to coast!
Now colic grips, and barkin' hoast
May kill us a';
For loyal Forbes' chartered boast
Is taen awa!

Thae curst horse-leeches o'th' Excise,
Wha mak the whisky stells their prize!
Haud up thy han', Deil! ance, twice, thrice!
There seize the blinkers!
An' bake them up in brunstane pies
For poor damn'd tinkers.

ROBERT BURNS

* hoast — cough; blinkers — spies.

The striking thing about her is that her imperiousness, which reminds me very much of Catherine the Great, or the Dragon Empress who presided over the terminal decline of the Manchu Dynasty in China — a thing for which you can find more women precedents than male precedents — is allied with a temperament which in many ways is very masculine, I mean when she's tired she'll head straight for the sideboard and pour herself a stiff whisky and soda . . .'

DENIS HEALEY, *THE THATCHER PHENOMENON*, RADIO 4, MAY 1985

A Reminiscence.

In the genial July weather,
Of 'ninety-nine' we started the 'Still'
There at the foot of Knock Candy's Hill;
'J.I.' and 'A.S' together.
Now this is the truth – not blether:
The "learners" we've been of good & ill
The 'Still' still stands a "Teacher's" Still.
'Neath the bonnie, purple heather.

Albert Smith J.R.

(Ardmore 1899 – 1911.)
Edin. 1/5/1916.

A page from the first autograph book of Miss Isabella J.R. Innes, daughter of James Innes, Manager of Glendronach Distillery and latterly the first Manager of Ardmore. This was given to the Chairman by Miss Innes in 1974. The "J.I." referred to is, of course, James Innes and "A.S." is Albert Smith the first Excise Officer at Ardmore. Both appear in the photograph of the original employees.

The Victorian traveller John Sands thoroughly recommended the Inn at Dunvegan because there are no other lodgings to be had. The goat-eyed landlord who talks both English and Gaelic as if an ear of barley had stuck in his throat is polite and courteous to your face. A rumour that fever raged on the premises caused them to be shunned by all except a few cattle-coupers who would have had their whisky although Death himself had acted as waiter and had brought in the stoups and glasses on a coffin lid.

Scotch whisky . . . is of the land and of time . . . Scotch whisky has become the drink of success, of fashion and prestige, drunk and appreciated by people of taste and discrimination all over the world.

From its humble origins on the hills and in the glens of Scotland, it has become the best-known international drink of all time. A bottle of Scotch in drunk every tenth of a second in the United States of America, a bottle a second in Venezuela, a bottle every seven seconds in Norway, a bottle every twenty seconds in the Philippines.

Each year Scotch whisky earns more than £700 million in the export markets of the world. And yet it remains true to its origins in the remote mountains and glens of Scotland, true to the traditions of patient skill and craftmanship handed down through the centuries, true to its name,
Uisge Beatha . . . the water of life.

EFFUSION FROM SCOTCH WHISKY ASSOCIATION

There was a woman down at the north end here and she had some friends at Castlebay. The Castlebay friends wrote her a note asking her to give the two children two bottles of whisky each. And she replied to the note, 'My dear Mary,' she said 'I am sorry I have no whisky today to give you. The last I had I bathed my feet in it, owing to the fact that I was severely bad with the rheumatism. But send down the children tomorrow and if all is well Donald will be at the *Polly* tonight and I am sure to be able to send you some.'

TALES FROM BARRA TOLD BY THE CODDY

The Politican ran ashore in 1941 on a small rock near Eriskay with a cargo of whisky destined for America. The locals salvaged it with enthusiasm.

Aberlour-Glenlivet est réputé tant comme pur malt que comme élément de base aux Scotch de cuvée les plus connus dans le monde.

CLAIM BY ABERLOUR'S OWNERS, THE SOCIÉTÉ PERNOD RICARD

10 gallons Glenlivet, 10 gallons Pitlochry, 5 gallons Reduced mixed Aqua, 8 gallons Grain, 4 gallons water, ½ gallon Aqua Shrub, 8 gallons Grain Aqua.

MIXTURE WHISKY, EXTRACT FROM WILLIAM SANDERSON'S RECORD BOOKS 1863, (HE FOUNDED WILLIAM SANDERSON LTD IN THAT YEAR)

Take of stale strong beer, or rather, the grounds thereof, put it into a copper still with a worm, distil it gently (or otherwise it will make the head of the still fly up) and there will come forth a weak spirit, which is called, low Wine: of which, when thou hast a good quantity, thou maist distil it again of itself, and there will come forth a good *Aqua Vitae.*

HOW TO MAKE *AQUA VITAE* OUT OF BEER, OLD RECIPE

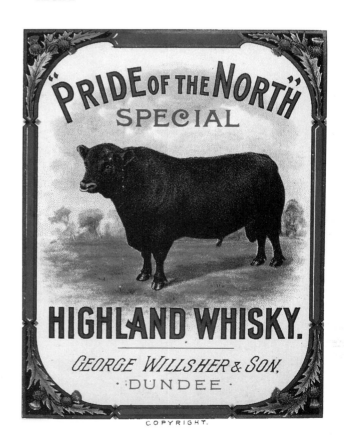

"PRIDE OF THE NORTH" SPECIAL

HIGHLAND WHISKY.

GEORGE WILLSHER & SON.
·DUNDEE·

COPYRIGHT.

O what lies younder north of Tweed?
Monsters, and hillmen — hairy kneed
And music that wad wauk the deid!
To venture there were risky O!

The fearsome haggis haunts the snaw
The kelpie waits — your banes to gnaw
There's nocht to eat but oatmeal — raw
BUT STILL I'M TOLD THERE'S WHISKY O!

ANON

Culloden is the most important date in the story of
whisky. It ruined the Jacobite chiefs and exalted the
Whigs who had supported the Hanoverians. It also
opened the Highlands to the Lowlands and the road
to the South. From now on whisky instead of being
what Burns called 'the poor man's wine' was to
become one more factory product.

SIR ROBERT BRUCE LOCKHART

Here's to a' your fouk an' a' oor fouk, an' a' the
fouk that's been kind to your fouk, an' a' the fouk
that's been kind to your fouk an' oor fouk; an' if a'
fouk had aye been as kind to fouk as your fouk's
been to our fouk, there wad aye hae been guid fouk
i' the warld, sin' fouk's been fouk.

TOAST OF THE OLD LANDLADY OF A LITTLE INN NOT
FAR FROM THE SCENE OF THE BATTLE OF
DRUMCLOG, WHEN SIR ARCHIBALD GEIKIE MADE
HER A GLASS OF TODDY

Just a wee deoch-an-dorius,*
Just a wee yin, that's a';
Just a wee deoch-an-doris
Before we gang awa.
There's a wee wifie waitin'
In a wee but an' ben;
If ye can say, 'It's a braw
    bricht moonlicht nicht',
Ye're a' richt, ye ken.

HARRY LAUDER (1870–1950)
* drink at the door

You whose ambition is to swim the Minch
Or write a drum concerto in B flat
Or run like Bannister or box like Lynch
Or find the Ark wrecked on Mt Ararat —
No special training's needed: thin or fat
You'll do it if you never once supplant
As basis of your commissariat
Glenfiddich, Bruichladdich and Glen Grant.

My own desires are small. In fact, I flinch
From heaving a heavenly Hindy from her ghat
Or hauling Loch Ness monsters inch by inch,
Out of their wild and watery habitat.
I've no desire to be Jehoshaphat
Or toy with houris fetched from the Levant.
But give to me — *bis dat qui cito dat* —
Glenfiddich, Bruichladdich and Glen Grant.

I would drink down, and think the feat a cinch,
The Congo, Volga, Amazon, La Platte,
And Tweed as chaser — a bargain, this, to clinch
In spite of *nota bene* and *caveat*
(Though what a feast must follow after that
Of Amplex, the divine deodorant!)
If they ran — hear my heart go pit-a-pit! —
Glenfiddich, Bruichladdich and Glen Grant.

   Envoi
Chris! (whether perpendicular or flat
Or moving rather horrible aslant)
Here is a toast that you won't scunner at:
Glenfiddich, Bruichladdich and Glen Grant!

BALLAD OF GOOD WHISKY, NORMAN MACCAIG

What are the most beautiful words in the English language? I asked the question one day in my *Sunday Times* column and offered bottles of champagne. One comedian, from a highly respectable Hampstead address, sent the following card: 'Glenfiddich, Glenlivet, Macallan, Glenmorangie, Glenfarclas and Clynelish'. Signed 'John Summerhill (hic)'.

GODFREY SMITH

Scotch is this island's noblest invention, the only one impossible to fake in Japan, mysteriously unique, at once oily and aflame, wholesome and dangerous, invigorating and numbing, a kind of heather-fed buttermilk gone mad. It is a defier of climates, and time zones. No Continental liqueur can match it neat, around 6 pm, after a day's touring across baked countryside, for burning off the frustrations of a carefree holiday. While on a wet night in London, diluted to the colour of weak tea, it becomes oddly super-potent at bedtime (always a good omen), mainlining itself into the bloodstream quicker than a blood transfusion.

ALAN BRIEN, *SUNDAY TIMES*

Is coisiche na h-oidhche thu
Gu leapannan na maighdeannan;
A Righ! gur h-iomadh loinn a th'ort
Gu coibhneas thoirt a gruagach.

You are the prowler of the night
To the beds of virgins;
O God! what powers you have
To gain kindness from girls.

A GAELIC TOAST QUOTED BY JAMES ROSS

When the last big bottle's empty and dawn creeps grey and cold,
And the last clan-tartan's folded and the last damned lie is told;
When they totter down the footpaths in a braw unbroken line,
To peril of the passers and the tune of 'Auld Lang Syne'
You can tell the folk at breakfast as you watch the fearsome sicht,
They've only been assisting at a braw Scots Nicht!

WILL OGILVIE

Bibliography

Alexander, Dr   *Northern Rural Sketches*

Ashford, Daisy   *The Young Visiters*. 1919

Barnard, Alfred   *The Whisky Distilleries of the United Kingdom*. Harper 1887

Bertram, J.G.   *Outdoor Sports in Scotland* 1889

Boswell, James   *Journal of a Tour to the Hebrides* 1785

Brander, Michael   *A Guide to Scotch Whisky*. Johnston & Bacon 1975

Briggs, E.E.   *Angling and Art in Scotland*

Brown, Ivor   *Summer in Scotland*. Collins

Burns, Robert   *Complete Poetical Works*

Burt, Edward   *Letters from a Gentleman in the North of Scotland to his friend in London*. 1754

Carr, Sir John   *Caledonian Sketches*

Carswell, Catherine and Donald   *The Scots Weekend*

Carus, Dr.   *The King of Saxony's Journey*

Cockburn, Lord   *Circuit Journeys*

Chadwick S.J.D. and Dudley H.A.F. *Can Malt Whisky be Discriminated* from *blended Whisky*? British Medical Journal. Vol 287 24–31 December 1983

Churchill, Winston   *A Roving Commission*

Collinson, Francis   *The Life and Times of William Grant*. 1979

Cooper, Derek   *The Century Companion to Whiskies. The Whisky Roads of Scotland*

Cousins, Geoffrey E.   *A Family of Spirit*. 1975

Critchley, Julian   *Westminster Blues*. Hamish Hamilton 1985

Craig, Elizabeth   *The Scottish Cookery Book*

Daiches, David   *Scotch Whisky*. Deutsch 1969

Dewar, Thomas   *A Ramble Round the Globe* 1904

Dickens, Cedric   *Drinking with Dickens*

Duncombe, David   *The Call To Duty*

Dunnet, A.M.   *The Land of Scotch*

Eden, Ronald   *Going to the Moors*. Murray 1979

Forbes Bishop   *Journal*

Forsyth, Robert   *The Beauties of Scotland* 1805

Garth   *Observations on Smuggling*

Geikie, Sir Archibald   *Scottish Reminiscences* 1904

Gillespie, Malcolm   *Memorial and Case of Malcolm Gillespie, Officer of Excise, Skene, Aberdeenshire*. Aberdeen 1826

Gordon Cumming, C.F.   *In the Hebrides*. 1886

Grant, Elizabeth   *Memoirs of a Highland Lady*

Gunn, Neil   *Whisky and Scotland. Young Art and Old Hector*

Healy, Maurice   *Stay Me With Flagons*

Henderson, John   *Annals of Lower Deeside*

Hislop, Alexander   *The Book of Scottish Anecdote*

House, Jack   *Pride of Perth*

Horner, Rev P.   *Observations on a Short Tour in the Summer of 1803 to the Western Highlands of Scotland*

House, Jack   *Scotch Whisky*

Hughes, Spike   in *The Compleat Imbiber* 1956

Jackson, Michael   *The World Guide to Whiskies*

Johnson, Samuel   *A Journey To the Western Islands of Scotland*

Keats, John   *The Letters of John Keats* edited by Maurice Buxton Forman. OUP 1931

Laver, James   *The House of Haig* 1958

Leyden, John   *Journal of a Tour to the Highlands in 1800*

Linklater, Eric   *The Lion and the Unicorn* 1935

Lockhart, J.G.   *Memoirs of the Life of Sir Walter Scott*

Lockhart, R. Bruce   *Scotch*. Putnam 1959

Macculloch, John   *A Description of the Western Islands* 1819

Macdonald, Aeneas   *Whisky*

Macdonald, Colin   *Echoes of the Glen*. Moray Press 1936

Macdonald, Ian   *Smuggling in the Highlands*. Inverness 1914

Mackenzie, Sir Compton   *Whisky Galore. My Life and Times. Octave Seven*

Mackenzie, Osgood Hanbury   *A Hundred Years in the Highlands*

Macpherson, John   *Tales From Barra Told by the Coddy*

Martin Martin   *A Description of the Western Highlands* 1703

Mitchell, James   *The Scotsman's Library* 1825

Mitchell, Joseph   *Reminiscences of My Life in the Highlands*

Montague, C.E.   *Fiery Particles*

Muir, Augustus   *Scottish Portrait*

Murphy, Brian   *The World Book of Whisky*

North, Christopher see Wilson, John

Pennant, Thomas *A Tour in Scotland and Voyage to The Hebrides* 1774

Ponsonby, Sir Frederick *Recollections of Three Reigns*

Pyke, Dr Magnus *Science and Scotch Whisky*

Ramsay, Dean *Scottish Life and Character* 1874

Ray, Cyril *Cognac*

Reeve-Jones, Alan *A Dram Life This*

Rogers, Rev Charles *Social Life in Scotland* 1884

Ross, James *Whisky*. RKP 1970

Saintsbury, George *Notes on a Cellar-Book* 1920

de Saussure, Necker *A Voyage to the Hebrides* 1822

Scott, Walter *St. Ronan's Well*

Scrope, William *Deer-stalking in the Scottish Highlands* 1838

Shand, Alexander Innes *Days of the Past* 1905

Smith, Alexander *A Summer in Skye* 1865

Smollett, Tobias *The Expedition of Humphry Clinker*

Stanhope, John *Journal* 1806

Stevenson, Robert Louis *Kidnapped*

Stewart of Garth *Sketches* 1825

Story, Rev Robert, *Memoirs*

Sutherland, Douglas *Raise Your Glasses*

Topham, Edward *Letters from Edinburgh* 1774–5

Troon, Anthony *Scotch Whisky* 1974

Walsh, Maurice *The Key Above The Door*

Waugh, Evelyn *Scoop*

Whittle, Tyler *Victoria and Albert At Home*. RKP 1980

Wilson, John *Noctes Ambrosianae*

Wordsworth, Dorothy *Recollections of a Tour in Scotland*

Index

Abbotsford 75
Aberdeen 16–17, 86
Aberfeldy 25, 54
Aberlour 33, 53, 120
Aberlour, Laird of 38
Agra 7
Albert, Prince Consort 42, 101, 103
Alexander, Dr 16
Allardes, James 47
Alloa 28
Allt a Bhainne 41
Alness 114
Angus, Braes of 20
Antiquary, The 33
aqua vitae 9, 28, 75, 120
Ardbeg 53, 64
Andmore 119
Ardrishaig 19
Argyll, Duke of 30
Ashford, Daisy 105
Aubrey, John 83
Auchorachan 38
Aultmore 54
Aytoun, W.E. 55

Baillie, Joanna 82
Baleiev, M. 115
Ballangich 17
Ballantine, George
Ballechin 54
Balmenach 12, 44, 54, 65
Balmoral castle 39, 42, 101–3
Balvenie 53
Banchory 75
Banff 45, 63
Banffshire Journal 47
Barleycorn, Sir John 8, 11, 45, 71, 72, 82, 83
Barnard, Alfred 12, 19, 23, 27, 29, 34, 40, 42, 43, 44, 45, 104
Barra, Isle of 97, 120
Barrie, Sir James 32
Begg, John 42, 101, 102
Bell, Arthur 33, 63, 108
Ben Nevis 54, 64, 102
Benmore 53
Ben Rinmes 20, 43, 44
Ben Rinnes 44, 45
Benromach 48, 54
bere 30, 84
Berry, Francis 34
Bertram, J.G. 89
Black Isle 57

Black & White whisky 32, 60
Blair Atholl 54
Blue Ribbon Army 78, 80
Boswell, James 87, 113
Bowmore 53
Brackla, Royal 42, 48, 53, 65
Braemar 16
Brander, Michael 106
Brechin 17, 54
Brien, Alan 115
Briggs, E.E. 107
Brora 48
Brown, Ivor 26, 59, 83, 110
Brown, John 102
Browne, Tom 51
Bruichladdich 41, 53, 122
Buchanan, Sir James 32, 60, 95, 96, 107
Bunnahabhainn 53
burials 7, 80, 105, 106
Burnfoot 14
Burns, Robert 7, 34, 71, 77, 82, 84, 85, 99, 118
Burntisland 65
Burt, Edward 94
Cairngorms 66
Callander 17, 80
Camlachie 39
Campbell, Hugh of Calder 106

Campbell, John Francis of Islay 96
Campbeltown 53, 78
Caol Ila 41, 53, 64
Cardow 53, 65, 82
Carr, Sir John 78
Carsebridge 48
Cawnpore 67
Chadwick, Stephen J.D. 63
Chisholm, The 11
Christie, James 107
Churchill, Sir Winston 81
Clynelish 53, 64, 65, 70, 92, 122
Cockburn, Lord 78−9, 106
cognac 77, 92
Coleburn 48, 53
Convalmore 48, 53
Conyngham, Lord 100
Cousins, Geoffrey E. 77
Coward, Noel 97
Cragganmore 41, 53
Craig, Elizabeth 20
Craigellachie 55
Crathie 42
Crieff 17, 54
Critchley, Julian 81
Cromdale 44
Crosland, T.W.H. 77
Cuillin hills 67, 92
Culloden 10, 36, 67, 105, 121
Culter 16
Cutty Sark 34
Daiches, David 7−8, 30, 56, 66, 68, 118
Dailuaine 45, 54
Dalintober 51, 53
Dallas Dhu 48, 54
Dalmore 53, 58
Dalwhinnie 53
Darjeeling 7
Dewar, Thomas 35, 41, 111, 112
Dickens, Cedric 33
Dingwall 15, 114
Disarming Act 10
Distillers Company 25, 31, 35, 45, 48, 109
Drumclog, Battle of 121
Dudley, Hugh A.F. 63
Dufftown 53

Dumbreck, Laird of 78
Duncombe, David 47
Dundee 77, 96, 120
Dunoon, Rev David 57
Dunvegan 119
Eden, Hon. Ronald 82
Edinburgh 90
Edradour 41, 53
Elgin 23
Erchless 11
Eriskay 120
Eunson, Magnus 104
Excise Act 10, 20, 38
excisemen 9, 11, 16, 17, 19, 20, 44, 57, 80
Fannich 18
Ferguson, Robert 80
Ferrier, Susan 94
Ferrintosh 36−7, 54, 62, 82, 118
Fettercairn 64
Fisher, Sir Ronald 63
Food, Ministry of 81
Forbes, Duncan of Culloden 36
Forsyth, Robert 64
Fort William 37, 94
Foster, William 117−8
Fraser, Dr of Kerrow 11
Fraser, Rev John 11
Fyffe, Will 58
Geikie, Sir Archibald 60, 78, 87, 91, 105, 112
George IV 100−1
Gillespie, Malcolm 16
Gladstone, William Ewart 102
Glen Albyn 48, 49, 55
Glenallachie 49
Glenburgie 49, 54, 65
Glencadam 49, 53
Glendarroch 19
Glendochart 107
Glendronach 42, 47, 49, 53, 64, 119
Glendullan 48, 49, 54
Glen Elgin 41, 49, 53
Glenesk 48, 49
Glenfarclas 40, 44, 49, 53, 122
Glenfiddich 22, 37, 49, 53, 63, 70, 122
Glenfoyle 49

Glenfyne 54
Glengarioch 49, 54
Glenglassaugh 49, 55
Glengoyne 49, 53
Glen Grant 49, 54, 64, 65, 70, 71, 117−8, 122
Glenkeith 41, 49
Glenkinchie 49
Glenleven 40
Glenlivet, The 7, 18, 23, 28, 29, 33, 38, 40, 42, 46, 47, 49, 54, 55, 64, 65, 70, 75, 91, 93, 96, 100, 108, 120, 122
Glenlochy 48, 49, 53
Glenlossie 49, 55, 65
Glen Mhor 48, 49, 54
Glenmorangie 49, 50, 54, 63, 118, 122
Glen Moray 49, 55
Glen Moray 49, 55
Glenquiech 20
Glenrothes 49, 54
Glen Scotia 49
Glenside 53
Glen Spey 49, 54
Glentauchers 48, 49, 54
Glenturret 41, 49, 54
Glenugie 41, 49, 55
Glenury 48, 49, 54
Gordon Cumming, C.F. 78
Gow, John 18
Gow, Neil 113
Grampians 17
Grandtully 45
Grange 65
Grant, Captain 'Bill' Smith 18
Grant, Elizabeth of Rothiemurchus 89, 100
Grant, Colonel Francis 100
Grant, Major James 117
Grant, John of Balnagowan 57, 111
Grant, John of Glenfarclas 44
Grant, S. Russell 28
Grant, Captain William 38, 49
Grant, Major William 37
Gunn, Neil 25, 60, 61−2, 65, 66, 67, 67, 70, 76
Guthrie, Rev. Thomas 17
Haig, Robert 11

Hamilton, Alan 92
Hay, Robert 44
Hazelburn 53
Healey, Denis 118
Healy, Maurice 67, 110
Heppenstall, Rayner 99
Highland Park 27, 40, 54, 65, 70, 104
Hislop, Alexander 105
Hogg, James 108
hogmanay 7, 115
Holinshed, Raphael 110
Horner, Rev P. 94
House, Jack 59, 77
Hughes, Spike 97
Humphries, Robert 34
Imperial 48, 55
Inchgower 42, 53, 77
Innes, James 119
Inverary 87
Inverewe 18
Inverness 86
Ireland 9
Islay 22−23, 31, 34, 41, 62, 64, 69, 70, 86, 96
Jackson, Michael 69
Jacobites 10, 121
John of Skye 75
Johnson, Dr. Samuel 87, 94
Johnston, Alexander 31
Jura 9
Kanchenjunga 7
Kavanagh, P.J. 93
Keats, John 99
Kelly, John 79
Kerrow 11
Kilbagie 71
Killearnan 87
Kiltarlity 11
Kinlochewe 87
Kintyre, Mull of 30, 53
Knockando 53, 118
Knockdhu 48, 54
Lagavulin 31, 40, 53, 64, 66
Lang Brothers 67
Laphroaig 23, 31, 53, 62
Lauder, Sir Harry 97, 121
Laver, James 66

Leyden, John 86
Linklater, Eric 60, 70
Linkwood 23, 48, 54, 65
Lloyd George, David 31, 59
Loch Etive 86
Lochmaree 44
Lochnagar 42, 54, 101, 103
Loch-nan-Uamh 67
Lochruan 51
Lochside 33
Lockhart, John Gibson 75, 100−1
Lockhart, Sir Robert Bruce 20, 49, 71, 84, 115, 121
Long John International 33
Longmorn 54, 65
Lustgarten, Edgar 97
Lyons, Agnes 113
Macadam, Dr Wilson 112
Macallan, The 30, 40, 53, 54, 65, 67, 122
Macbey, James 34
MacCaig, Norman 122
McCarthy, Desmond 98
Macculloch, John 83, 87
Macdiarmid, Hugh 64, 108−9, 116
Macdonald, Aeneas 55, 65, 71, 83, 118
Macdonald of Borrodale 67
Macdonald, Colin 15, 111
Macdonald, John of Strathpeffer 15
Macdonald, Ian 11, 114
Macdonald, Long John 37, 74, 102
Macdonald Martin Distilleries 40
McDougall, Alexander 34
McGonagall, William 80
Macgregor 20
MacGregor, Sandy 11
Machrie 66
M'Ian of Skye 79
MacIan, Robert Ronald 11
Mackall, Lawton 84
Mackenzie, Sir Compton 83, 97−8
Mackenzie, David 58
Mackenzie, Dr. John 18
Mackenzie, Osgood Hanbury 18
Mackenzie, Roderick 23
McKessek, Dougie 117−8
Mackie, Sir Peter 31, 39
Mackie, Philip 97

Mackinlay, Donald 26
Mackinlay's Whisky 58
Macleod, Mary 113
Macmillan, Father John 97
Macnab Distilleries 50
Madam Butterfly 97
Mahoney, Jack 68
Malt Mill 53
Mannochmore 48
Mar, Braes of 18
Margaret, HRH Princess 102
Martin Martin 28
Meg Dods 115
Millburn 48, 53
Miltonduff 55
Minmore 18
Mitchell, James 29, 37
Mitchell, Joseph 14, 67
Montague, C.E. 113
Mortlach 45, 53, 56
Muir, Augustus 69, 80, 91, 116
Murphy, Brian 71
Nevis 42
New Scientist 26
Nicolson, Jessie 91
North, Christopher 108
North Port 48, 54
Northern Rural Sketches 16
Oban 53
Ogilvie, Will 123
Orkney 9, 27, 43, 54, 104
Orwell, George 56
Patti, Adelina 95
Pattisons' Whisky 79
Paul, Saunders 75
Pennant, Thomas 30
Phillips, Willie 30
Playfair, Dr 110
Politician, S.S. 120
Ponsonby, Sir Frederick 103
Port Ellen 48, 53
Port Dundas 48
Pulteney 54, 68
Pyke, Dr. Magnus 28
Ramsay, Dean 75, 80
Ray, Cyril 76
revenue men 9, 12, 19

Richmond, Duke of 38
Ricketts, Rev Harry 64
Rieclachan 53
Robertson, John of Crathie 42
Rogers, Rev Charles 95, 106
Ross, James 123
Ross, William 35
Rothes 117
St. Andrews 80
St. Giles Edinburgh 104
St. Magdalene 48
St. Ninian 11
Saintsbury, George 65, 70
Sanderson, William 55, 120
Sands, John 119
de Saussure, Necker 14
Scapa 41, 54
Scotch Whisky Association 58, 119
Scotia 53
The Scotsman 33
Scott, Sir Walter 75, 82, 100–1, 108
Scottish Royal Academy 11
Scottish Tourist Board 93
Scrabster 61
Scrope, William 83, 87
Seagrams 33
Shand, Alexander Inmes 86, 91
Sharman, Howard 51
Shaw, Ned 77
Sherrif, Andrew 84
Skene 16
Skye, Isle of 23, 68, 91, 92, 105, 113, 119
Smith, Alexander 37, 39, 82

Smith, George & J.G. 18, 29, 38, 64, 65
Smith, Godfrey 122
Smollett, Tobias 91, 105, 113
smugglers and smuggling 9, 10, 11, 12–13, 14, 15, 16, 17, 18, 19, 28, 42, 43, 60
Smythe, Dame Ethel 97
Speyburn 54
Spiller, Brian 45
Springbank 53, 63
Standfast 43
Stanhope, John 94, 111
Stein, John 9
Stevenson, Robert Louis 9, 114, 116
Stirling 17, 18
Stirling, Edward 96
Stonebyres 8
Story, Rev. Robert 106
Strathallen, Lord 105
Strathblane 14
Strath Bran 18
Strathisla 54
Strathmill 54
Strathpeffer 15
Stromness 43, 54
Stuart, Prince Charles Edward 18, 67, 105
Tain 114
Taj Mahal 7
Talisker 23, 37, 55, 64, 65, 67, 68, 91
Tamdhu 53,
Teacher, William & Sons 33, 52, 76–7, 118

Teaninich 48, 53
Thatcher, Margaret 118
Thomas, Dylan 99
Tiree 86
Tobermory 55
Tomatin 41, 53
Tomintoul 18
Tomintoul 41
Topham, Edward 90
Tormore 41
trestarig 28
Troon, Anthony 33, 64
Tudge, Colin 26
Twain, Mark 84
uisge beatha 7, 10, 28, 72, 82, 109, 119
Ullapool 87
Usher, Andrew 39
VAT 69 55, 56
Victoria, Queen 39, 44, 101–3
Walker, Professor 19
Walker, Johnnie 33, 51, 55, 78, 95
Walsh, Maurice 28, 30, 42–3, 70, 92
Waugh, Evelyn 95
weddings 7
Wester Ross 23
White Horse Inn 5
White Horse whisky 31, 41, 51, 59, 63, 109
Whittle, Tyler 102
William IV, 15
Wilson, John 108
Wordsworth, Dorothy 88